PLAYS

Ghosts of Valparaiso
A Play in Two Acts

and

Conversations with James
A Comedy in Six Acts

Andre Vltchek

BADAK MERAH SEMESTA

2014

PLAYS

Ghosts of Valparaiso

and

Conversations with James

Copyright © 2014 Andre Vltchek

All rights reserved

Written by: Andre Vltchek

Preface by: Gaither Stewart and Patrice Greanville

Edited by: Tony Christini

Cover Design and Layout by: Rossie Indira

Cover & Portrait Photos by: Alejandro Wagner

First edition, 2014

Published by PT. Badak Merah Semesta, Jakarta

http:/badak-merah.weebly.com

email: badak.merah.press@gmail.com

ISBN: 978-602-70058-5-3

Plays

Andre Vltchek

TABLE OF CONTENTS

PREFACE ix

GHOSTS OF VALPARAISO

   ACT ONE

      Scene One 1

      Scene Two 13

      Scene Three 23

      Scene Four 29

      Scene Five 35

   ACT TWO

      Scene Six 51

      Scene Seven 69

      Scene Eight 81

      Scene Nine 93

CONVERSATIONS WITH JAMES

    PREFACE 121

    ACT ONE 129

    ACT TWO 141

    ACT THREE 155

    ACT FOUR 165

    ACT FIVE 173

    ACT SIX.................................... 179

About the Author 195

Compliments for Andre Vltchek..... 199

Plays

Andre Vltchek

PREFACE

As artists from Sophocles to Camus were the living testimony, writing a political play is as difficult an undertaking for a writer as it is irresistible. With every word, with every line, the playwright is tiptoeing his way through a mine field, forever wavering between a political treatise on the one side and a propagandistic banality on the other.

From the first line of the first scene to the closing words of the final scene the author walks on a razor's edge, the theatrical-literary on one side, propaganda on the other, while the dramatist in reality is thinking in tragic, philosophic, theoretical, historical terms.

The history of social realism, whose origins can be traced to the French revolution, and whose impulse yielded a rich crop of 19th and 20th century painters, writers and playwrights, including a powerful and influential American contingent, and which later, in a more self-conscious, pronounced way, infused socialist realism, is something of a cautionary tale.

Despite enormous and well deserved successes such as Eisenstein's Alexander Nevsky (1938), whose script was co-written with the gifted Pyotr Pavlenko, moral didactic plays are an artistically elusive form. In most cases the feat is difficult, if not well-nigh impossible. Indeed the frequent failures we saw during the period of socialist realism in theater and cinema plays, and later in the well-intentioned but ultimately clumsy attempts by postwar Western Marxian activists and leftwing writers to educate (and inspire) the masses through scripts that presented poorly drawn characters overwhelmed by symbolic didacticism, constantly spewing the "correct line", ended up losing audiences not so much through ideological resistance as simple boredom. However, when the exceptions hit the mark they leave an imprint not easily forgotten, and Vltchek is exceptional.

Vltchek shows in his political play, *Ghosts of Valparaiso*, you cannot be free against the unfreedom of others. But how to be free remains the unanswered and perhaps the unanswerable question. Camus' Theatre, for example, leads the reader to believe that every person bears within himself a portion of illusion, but that the best part of man is that of the revolt that leads to freedom. Inevitably in every literary debate in the end what kind of freedom becomes the question. And for whom. Likewise, Camus' The Just, set in Moscow in 1906, probes the motives and conflicts of a group of revolutionaries planning a political assassination, which the writer executes without falling into the trap of literature as propaganda.

The complex and bewildering story of Sophocles' Antigone is the polarization of one of the basic elements of the relationship between man and society—the individual's challenge to Power ... and Power's reaction to that challenge. The confrontation between Antigone and King Creon reflects the dialectics of Western society since the time of the ancient Greeks in all its political, social, moral and legal ramifications. The reading I give to the tragedy is socio-political—the individual vs. Power. Since the ancient Greeks, Antigone's challenge to power has been repeated down through the centuries as people have risked all for personal freedom.

The challenges facing André Vltchek in the composition of Ghosts of Valparaiso were great, which, during the reading, bewildered me, hesitations as a rule overcome by the author's use of delayed revelations in good theatrical style--by an apparent love affair being born on the stage, by suggestions of realistic sound effects, and by the supernatural quality of the ghosts of the past which I will not reveal here.

Vltchek's impassioned accusations of political crimes against humanity perpetrated by the USA, the West, NATO come through clear, as they should, in the words of both the ghosts and the survivors, as well as the author's hopes for and appeals to the rest of the world to resist and to be ready to answer the call to go to barricades in defense of the rest of mankind.

In Sophocles, the Chorus, that is the

public and society, discerning or not, vacillates in its support, first for the man of State and Power, then for the higher right. For the Chorus, Antigone is less than human. She is one who no longer counts, somewhere out of the world, a substratum, to be compared to the unconsidered masses, non-represented, non-participating, non-voting majority of the world who have no role in the exercise of Power. At the end of Sophocles' tragedy, one wonders which gods and what kind of gods they are all appealing to if they all believe they are acting within the mandate of the gods. However that may be, Creon, the King, is the representative of arbitrary Power which the oppressed, for whatever their reasons, have the divine right to doubt, question and bring down.

Freedom requires that man act polemically, precisely in order to realize himself and to bring about a just society. In order to reject the fatalism that leads us to accept that what will come to pass will come to pass. People die but others must go on. This is the "thin line" of decency and civilization which both Erasmus and Voltaire praised in their writings, and which in each epoch somehow manages to resist (successfully) the assaults of barbarism, or merely survive to fight again another day. That they exist is indeed the ultimate miracle. As many have wondered before, where do such people come from?

Gaither Stewart

and

Patrice Greanville

Plays

Andre Vltchek

GHOSTS OF VALPARAISO

A Play in Two Acts

MAIN CHARACTERS

Diego

Niar and Asian Lady (performed by the same actress)

Father

Mother

Waiter

Laura and Victoria (performed by the same actress)

1st SOLDIER

2nd SOLDIER

Girl Student

Boy Student

Andre Vltchek

SCENES

ACT ONE

Scene One: Large and bare room, some unnamed war torn country in Southeast Asia, probably in Indonesia, in a small and remote provincial capital. Country is invaded by the US troops. Time: late morning or early afternoon.

Scene Two: Valparaiso; one of the old fashioned bars in this historical Chilean port city. Time: the same day as SCENE ONE; approximately the same hour.

Scene Three: The same as SCENE ONE but several hours later.

Scene Four: The same as Scene Three, immediately after

Scene Five: The same time and place as in Scene Four

ACT TWO

Scene Six: The same as SCENE TWO but several weeks later.

Scene Seven: Dining room in some old house in Valparaiso.

Scene Eight: Same as Scene Six, immediately after Scene Seven.

Scene Nine: Same as Scene Eight, immediately after.

THERE WILL BE NO INTERMISSION

ACT ONE

Andre Vltchek

SCENE ONE

SCENE: *Large room in a rustic house, neat and clean but bare; a bed on the left side of the stage. Two chairs but no table and one lamp hanging from the ceiling. The door on the right side is always shut. The wall clock, which doesn't move, is stuck at 12 o'clock.*
The stage is illuminated by dim lights.

DIEGO, a Chilean reporter in his early forties, unshaved for several days, is naked from the waist up, his left arm covered by bandage.

NIAR, an Asian woman, can be in her early or late thirties, well groomed, wearing a long dress. Her head is covered and the scarf itself is elegant, decorated by a single pearl.

DIEGO is asleep. NIAR is sitting next to him on the bed, motionless. Suddenly his body shakes. He sits up, breaths heavily, his eyes closed. After a while his eyes open; he doesn't look at her, but looks straight ahead.

NIAR (*touching his arm, gently*)

It's all right. Lie down. Lie down...

DIEGO: Eh?

(*Realizing that he is not alone, he looks at her. Recognizing her, he breathes a sigh of relief*)

Niar...

NIAR: Yes. Me. Niar... It's me.

DIEGO: (*whispers*)

You... the girl from the hotel... a manager... before the place got blown sky-high.

(*He wipes the sweat from his forehead, leaning towards her, quietly*)

I had a nightmare...

NIAR: Sorry?

DIEGO: A nightmare. Bad dream, you know...?

NIAR: Bad dream... yes. I understand. But

I am here. Don't you worry...

DIEGO: Yes.

(*Silence, then explosion, far away; then another and another. Could be the sound of continuous artillery fire. Diego nods towards the explosions*)

It's getting closer.

NIAR: Sometimes it goes away... It sounds remote, sometimes. Then it comes back again.

DIEGO: And now?

NIAR: (*She listens*)

I don't know. I think it's getting closer. I'm not sure.

(*She straightens her headscarf*)

When it comes very close, they will move in. You'll be able to go home, Diego.

DIEGO: Home... Yes. And you too will be able to leave this house and go wherever you want.

NIAR: I have nowhere else to go. They destroyed the hotel. This is my house.

DIEGO: You could try to find your family.

NIAR: I would be afraid to leave this place. And my family... they may not be...

DIEGO: (*Falls back to bed; interrupts her*)

Don't say it!

NIAR: I won't.

(*She sits next to him, her body erect, motionless. Diego tries to get hold of her hand. She hesitates for just a moment, then withdraws her hand*)

DIEGO: I'm sorry.

NIAR: Don't apologize. It's me. Forgive me. I'm not used to being touched.

(*Diego sits up in bed again. They remain very close to each other, apparently confused*)

DIEGO: Now I can remember everything very clearly. We were talking in the lobby of your hotel as we had been for almost two days. Then the hotel was hit, everything collapsed. I remember feeling terrible pain, then nothing. I lost consciousness. When I woke up, you were next to me. What surprised me was that your clothes were clean; you looked as if nothing had happened. There was no lobby, no hotel, anymore. But you still looked the same. Then you brought me here. I could hardly walk and I had to lean on you...

NIAR: You were so heavy. I didn't know that a man could be so heavy...

DIEGO: Before we entered your house, you let me rest on a bench. You went to the garden behind the corner and you suddenly screamed... You cried. What had you seen?

NIAR: Nothing... I saw nothing at all, Diego.

DIEGO: Then I don't remember anything.

NIAR: You slept for almost twenty hours.

DIEGO: I was exhausted. I haven't slept for two nights before.

NIAR: And you are injured.

DIEGO: It's nothing, just some scratches.

(*Several explosions, one after another, then silence*)

Thank you.

NIAR: Don't mention it.

(*Light goes off*)

Again!

(Another explosion, this time nearby)

DIEGO: Why are they bombing this town?

(Electricity goes back on)

NIAR: *(Sarcastically)*

They say that it's full of Muslim fundamentalists.

DIEGO: Is it?

NIAR: The Americans say we are hiding people that they are searching for.

DIEGO: But... nobody is shooting back.

NIAR: Because there is nobody here, anymore. The people escaped. Or they are dead.

DIEGO: *(abruptly sits down)*

Nobody left...? Just the two of us...?

NIAR: Nobody, Diego... just you and me.

(The light blinks. Niar looks at Diego. Her face is illuminated by a weak ray of blue light. Her expression changes but it lasts for several seconds only. The light stops blinking and her face relaxes)

Are you afraid?

DIEGO: (*hesitates*)

No, not at all...

NIAR: Good.

DIEGO: And now... what are we going to do?

NIAR: Nothing. We will wait.

DIEGO: Wait for what?

NIAR: (*Abruptly*)

Simply wait!

(*Her voice softens*)

We'll wait until your people come, Diego. Wait until they come...

DIEGO: My people? They are not my people, Niar. I'm a Chilean writer, a journalist. Chile... It's not in the United States...

NIAR: It's in America...

DIEGO: South America. If you flew from New York to Santiago de Chile, it would take you more than ten hours. Almost as far as from here to Paris.

NIAR: I see. I'm sorry. We don't know much about that part of the world here.

DIEGO: (*He tries to get off the bed but is suddenly overwhelmed by pain. He sits on the bed, holding his shoulder*)

It hurts...

NIAR: Stay put, Diego. Stay in bed.

DIEGO: No, not that... it hurts that we don't know anything about each other.

NIAR: I am just a simple woman...

DIEGO: No you're not. We spoke for two days, remember? You are bright. We understood each other... intuitively...

NIAR: If you say so...

DIEGO: (*Hesitates, than speaks*)

When all this will be over... one day...

NIAR: Yes?

DIEGO: Will you come to my city? I didn't grow up there. I grew up with my grandmother in France, but that's beside the point. I'll tell you my story later. But now I feel like going back to my city and I want you to come with me, to visit me there. Will you come... please?

NIAR: You know my country and you know the answer, so why do you ask? We're not rich, Diego. People here don't travel just like that. After you leave, we will never see each other again.

DIEGO: (*This time he succeeds in getting up. He stands up, then bends, holding on to the frame of the bed*)

That's not true!

(*Niar is silent, motionless*)

We will not part like this. You saved my life. You carried me through the ruins of the hotel to your home, through the burning city.

(*Excited*)

I won't leave like this. You have become like my sister, like...

(*Niar extends her hand and covers his mouth with her palm*)

NIAR: Hush, silly.

(*She smiles at him, tenderly*)

Don't speak...

DIEGO: (*sits down next to her*)

I want to take you to my city. I want you to walk with me through its hills. I want you to meet the people that I love and to tell you all about the people that I lost...

NIAR: What's the name of your city?

DIEGO: Valparaiso.

NIAR: What does it mean?

DIEGO: When the Spanish conquerors arrived, they saw a big bay surrounded by steep hills. They looked up and one of them said "It's like going to heaven". "Va-al-paraiso..."

NIAR: That's beautiful.

DIEGO: It's what the legend says. And the city itself is beautiful... but not in an ordinary way.

(Loud explosion)

It's very sad. It's a city of poets and ghost stories, of narrow, almost Arabic streets, of millions of cats and century old cable-cars. It's a city of fishermen and of dreamers, of fog and of huge ships arriving from all over the world. It's very melancholic city; very poor, but full of pride and dignity.

NIAR: *(Dreamily)*

I would like to visit your city. Cable-cars you said? And cats?

DIEGO: I'll take you there.

(Distant roar of helicopter engines)

NIAR: But it's on the other side of the world.

DIEGO: It doesn't matter.

(Two powerful explosions)

NIAR: *(Suddenly determined, looking straight at him)*

Then take me there, Diego. Take me there now, if you dare! Let's go, before it's too late.

(He comes closer to her, he embraces her. She tries to push him away but suddenly changes her mind. She lets her head drop. Her head is pushing against his naked chest. They stay like this for several seconds)

BLACKOUT

Andre Vltchek

SCENE TWO

Scene: *Old bar in Valparaiso. Could be "J-Cruz" or any similar place in downtown. It looks almost like an antique store with an antique cash register, ancient objects and empty bottles with strange colors and shapes. A very old bolero, "Encadenados" by Lucho Gatica, is playing in the background. Two couples are dancing, another couple is sitting at the table holding hands, talking.*

Diego and Niar enter. Niar is still wearing her headscarf, but her dress is light and elegant and she is also wearing light summer sandals.

They sit down at a table in the middle of the bar.

NIAR: What lovely music!

DIEGO: Shall we dance?

NIAR: Yes... No. Wait.

(*They look straight at each other*)

Diego...?

DIEGO: (*Takes her hand between his palms. Laughing*)

Yes?

NIAR: I think this place makes me happy.

DIEGO: (*Still laughing*)

But you look almost frightened!

NIAR: It's not that. I guess I didn't know how it feels... Forgive me. Let's not talk about it and please don't laugh at me.

DIEGO: I'm not laughing at you. I'm laughing because I'm happy, too.

NIAR: And why are you happy?

DIEGO: Because you are here, because I am back in Chile – with you...because the sun is shining outside and because your hands are warm.

(*Suddenly serious*)

Because I hope that you will stay with me; because this may be our beginning...

(*The music stops*)

NIAR: Do you really believe in happy endings?

DIEGO: Yes. I believe in happy ending to this story.

NIAR: (*smiles at him, tenderly and sadly*)

You are such a child, Diego.

(*A waiter in black trousers, white shirt and a black jacket serves wine for Diego and a large glass of juice for Niar*)

WAITER: (*smiles at them*)

Beautiful day, isn't it?

DIEGO: Yes. Not one cloud outside.

WAITER: (*to Niar*)

You come from far away, madam?

NIAR: Yes. I come from an island nation... from Asia, from far, far away.

WAITER: Then welcome to Valparaiso. It's an honor to have you here.

(*Nodding at Diego*)

I've known this boy since he was so little he could easily hide under one of those tables. Then one day he left; he disappeared for many years. Once in a while, he would return, but just for a short time. And now he is back... with you.

(*Dreamily*)

I can detect the scent of the sea and that of tropical flowers. It's evaporating from your skin.

DIEGO: (*laughing*)

Are you also a poet, brother?

WAITER: (*without smiling*)

Of course I am. Here, we are all poets. Valparaiso is a city of poets and ghosts. But I am not a ghost.

(*Waiter leaves. Someone starts to play a piano off stage. It is some old tango. The lights become dimmer. The two couples continue to dance*).

NIAR: My feet are hurting me, but I feel so light. You showed me 'Cerro Allegre' and 'Cerro Concepcion'. We took the old Turi cable car - it was rocking on the old rails and we were screaming and laughing, being pulled higher and higher... and then I saw the port, the bay, hundreds of ships. We drank coffee at café Brighton and then you took me to the old fishermen's wharf for lunch. We climbed aboard an old blue trolley-bus: we were the only passengers and the driver gave us a big smile. And then, in the middle of some narrow street, you kissed me, Diego. I had never been kissed before and I felt like I was fainting, so I held on to you, and you kept kissing me, and I closed my eyes and then opened them again... and you were still there...

DIEGO: And we took the taxi all the way up, almost to the top of the hill, to La Sebastiana – one of the houses that used to belong to Pablo Neruda...

NIAR: It was so high. Looking from the window of his bedroom I felt that I was sailing and flying at the same time. It's where he slept, where he embraced Matilda, his wife, his last love. And far away, I could see the white snow-covered peaks of the enormous Andes. And you read me a poem...

DIEGO: So, this is my city, Niar, or at least it used to be my city, many years ago. And coming back with you, it feels that it's mine again... and yours.

NIAR: And my country is yours, too. Don't you miss it, at least a little?

DIEGO: I do, tremendously.

NIAR: They complement each other, don't they? Pity one can't live in two places...

DIEGO: One can.

NIAR: I feel happy here. But I already miss the deep silence of the nights at home, the smell of flowers, so overwhelming and so reassuring... spices and powerful colors...my language and the tranquil surface of the sea...the music.

DIEGO: I miss it, too. But there is a war there...

NIAR: Don't speak about it now!

(*She takes his hand*)

But Diego... I just realized... where I come from... We have big families. We live together. Today you showed me streets and cable cars, cats and markets, churches and the port of Valparaiso. But I saw hardly any people. I didn't see your mother or your father, Diego. I didn't see your brothers and sisters...

(*The lights get even dimmer, then blackout. A few seconds later, one single spotlight illuminates the old photo on the wall, depicting a burning presidential palace 'La Moneda' in Santiago de Chile*).

DIEGO: Niar?

NIAR: Yes?

(It is impossible to see their faces. The music stops. The two couples are still dancing but now only their shadows are visible)

DIEGO: Can you be my mother..? And my sister..? And my wife..?

NIAR: Yes, yes... Yes I can, I am... but wait... What are you talking about?

DIEGO: Don't you understand?

NIAR: No... forgive me...

DIEGO: God, you grew up so far away from Chile. You don't know what happened to me, do you?

NIAR: No. I know nothing. Only what you were showing me today... and it was so beautiful, so serene...

DIEGO: *(sighs)*

Well then...

(Total blackout... Then red and orange lights start criss-crossing the stage. A woman begins to scream. Sounds of gun-fire outside, loud explosions, helicopter engines

roaring. People start moving the tables frantically, scratching the floor, then absolute silence. Dim lights come back)

IMPERSONAL METALLIC PRE-RECORDEDVOICE: Today, on September 11, 1973, Chilean armed forces left their barracks and took over control of the capital city. The presidential palace, 'La Moneda', is burning. Salvador Allende, democratically elected socialist President of Chile is presumed dead. According to eyewitness reports he refused to leave, proudly and defiantly walking towards the soldiers, armored vehicles and helicopter gun-ships, towards his certain end. One of the oldest democracies on earth collapsed. The coup had been orchestrated and sponsored by various North American companies and by the government of the United States. Henry Kissinger summarized his government's position by declaring: "I see no reason why a certain country should be allowed to go Marxist merely because its people are irresponsible".

(As the voice fades, there is a long pause. The lights are still dim as before, then blackout. One single, strong light illuminates the center of the stage.

Suddenly a big, strong man, blindfolded, his hands tied behind his back, is thrown to the middle of the stage. His face is covered by blood. So is his wide-open white shirt. He kneels in the centre of the stage, but looks defiantly straight ahead at the audience)

DIEGO: My father!

(Blackout. The man disappears. Once again, a strong single light illuminates the center of the stage. A woman is thrown to the floor, her long black hair loose, her blouse torn open exposing her bra, her skirt half ripped, with blood running down her legs and feet. She falls to the floor, looking at the audience, her facial expression that of pain, desperation, humiliation and horror.

DIEGO: *(leaning towards Niar)*

My mother!

(Silence for 10 seconds, than blackout. One single gunshot in the darkness)

My older brother...

(The blackout lasts for 10 more seconds. Then all lights back on. The same scene as before: Café, two couples dancing, but no music. Niar is looking at Diego, speechless, with tremendous compassion).

DIEGO: You are all I have.

BLACKOUT

Andre Vltchek

SCENE THREE

(Exactly the same settings at SCENE 1. Almost complete darkness. Two children – a boy and a girl – are laughing behind the stage. Their voices can be pre-recorded. Niar and Diego are asleep. Diego sleeps under the cover, Niar on top of the blanket. They are both dressed and Niar's head is still covered by the scarf)

FIRST CHILD: Auntie Niar!

SECOND CHILD: Wake up, auntie Niar!

(Light slowly increases)

NIAR: *(Wakes up. She stares ahead of her for a short while then jumps off the bed, towards the voices:)*

Where are you?

CHILDREN: Auntie Niar, auntie Niar... Why don't you follow us?

NIAR: (*searching for the direction from which the voices are coming. Confused*)

I can't... I can't...

CHILDREN: We're waiting for you... waiting for you... waiting for you... All of us are waiting for you.

NIAR: No! Please go. Go!

(*With tremendous difficulty she starts to back up, towards the bed*)

CHILDREN: Stay then, but we will soon come back... we will come back for you...

DIEGO: (*wakes up*)

Niar!

NIAR: (*falls on top of the bed. Pushes the blanket aside and presses her forehead into his chest*)

My love!

DIEGO: (*First shocked, but then quickly embraces her, caressing her shoulders*)

What did you just say?

NIAR: We returned.

DIEGO: Returned?

NIAR: Yes, returned; from Valparaiso.

DIEGO: (*slowly*)

Niar, have you had the same dream?

NIAR: Yes, yes. But was it really a dream? The music... what was the name of the song?

(*She is humming "Encadenados"*)

And the poem you read to me in Pablo Neruda's house.

DIEGO: "Your smile".

NIAR: Yes.

DIEGO: Niar, I heard some voices. I woke up because someone was calling your name. One or two children... Who are they?

NIAR: That was nothing.

DIEGO: Or maybe I was still dreaming...

(*Enormous explosion... sound of shattered glass. Diego pulls Niar closer to him. Their lips meet, just for a single moment. Then she gently pushes him away*)

NIAR: I can't here. Somebody might see us...

DIEGO: But you said that nobody was left in this town.

NIAR: I know, I know... I just can't.

(*She buries her face in the pillow. A short while after, her entire body starts to shake. Diego is motionless*)

You hardly know me. I'm a Muslim. I don't drink wine. I don't know anything about your country, except what you showed me...

DIEGO: (*smiles*)
We can both learn.

NIAR: (*she interrupts him*)

We don't even speak the same language...

(*Bitterly*)

And soon we will start declaring our love in the language of the occupiers...

DIEGO: It's the language of Shakespeare and Byron, of Faulkner and Hemingway. It's a good language; all languages are good. What is happening outside has nothing to do with the language.

(Her shoulders keep shaking)

Why? Why are you crying now?

NIAR: *(hesitates, then speaks)*

For Salvador Allende... and for your father, Diego... and for your mother and for your brother... and for myself!

BLACKOUT

Andre Vltchek

SCENE FOUR

(The same settings as the previous SCENE 3. Niar and Diego sitting on two chairs, opposite each other)

NIAR: *(She doesn't talk to anyone in particular; it is as if she is in her own universe, although Diego responds and there is some sort of dialogue)*

You took me to Buenos Aires. We left Santiago de Chile at dawn. We drove on the new highway, bypassing the city of Los Andes. The road was passing through enormous vineyards, orchards and gardens; we saw horses and meadows at the side of the mountains. Then the road started to climb. We were following a river with crystal clear water. It was ice cold, jumping over the boulders. And then, suddenly, I saw the mountains in all their beauty; enormous, their peaks covered by snow.

(Her voice suddenly changes)

You said they were dropping prisoners from the helicopters onto the mountains...

DIEGO: Yes, and also into the ocean. But before dropping them they cut their stomachs open, so they wouldn't float on the surface... But they were still alive...

(Short pause, then she continues with the previous voice)

NIAR: I saw Mount Aconcagua, on the border between Chile and Argentina, almost seven thousand meters high, with one small cloud caressing its summit. Diego, you stopped the car and we walked through the grass so fresh and so green... You showed me another river. "That one flows in the opposite direction", you said. "All Chilean rivers flow into the Pacific. Argentinean rivers head towards the Atlantic." We saw fantastic rocks and minerals and hot springs. We drove to Mendoza, to the first big city in Argentina, surrounded by vineyards. It looked so green, serene and welcoming. When you told me that the people there were starving, I couldn't believe it. Then you drank wine and I drank grape juice, so sweet and delicious. There was so much life on the streets at night, so much music in the streets and cafes, wide branches of trees. I thought I was in Paris.

DIEGO: We made love there... the first time...

NIAR: *(jumps from her chair, happy. Paces around the room, her voice excited, her speech fast)*

Then, after making love, we walked into the middle of the night. People were still on the streets. There was a huge fountain and the water was constantly changing its shape and color. And there was music everywhere. And street artists... people sipping hot tea from the metal straws attached to their cups...

DIEGO: They call it jerba... jerba mate...

NIAR: Yes, and I tried and it was so bitter and the woman who offered it to me was laughing at my grimace... The people were so nice. They tried to start a conversation. But I didn't understand, so they just smiled at me. And then I saw several posters; photos of my country on them, a red color like blood covering the image of my capital city... And some students tried to explain something to me and then there was this woman in her sixties, she said that she lost her son during the dictatorship. She asked me where I came from and when I told her, she embraced me, she held me for several minutes and kept repeating: "We will not allow it this time, my child... Never again..."

DIEGO: The whole continent of South America is on the edge, Niar. The war in your country, the invasion and resistance of your people inspired the people here. Protesters are clashing with the police. Students are throwing stones at the windows of the US embassies. There are riots; in Argentina, in Brazil, in Chile... And In Mexico City, hundreds of thousands of protesters are demanding immediate withdrawal of their country from NAFTA. I never saw such solidarity before. People are waking up...

NIAR: Yes, yes... But my time with you was so limited... I couldn't, I didn't want to think about anything except us. The next day we drove to Buenos Aires, through the endless flatlands...

DIEGO: Through the pampas...

NIAR: ...and I... I fell in love with that city at first sight.

(She stops. Music of Piazolla, not very loud, only as a background)

You took me to the old Teatro Colon... And then we walked the whole night, from café to café, from bar to bar, through that majestic city. We went to the neighborhood of Santelmo, to small and cozy places where people dance the tango... We danced, too, clumsily. I suddenly wanted you so much, Diego... I couldn't wait any longer. Our hotel was in the center - so far away from Santelmo. We rented a room in a small pension with only one bed and sink and a window facing the courtyard...

DIEGO: And we stayed until the morning, without sleeping one single minute.

NIAR: The next day we ate fresh, crispy *churos*, dipping them in hot chocolate. Then you said that I saw but a fraction of this enormous continent and I interrupted, I said that I love you, like a silly woman who is really in love for the first time in her life...

(Enormous explosion and the sound of falling debris. Then silence)

DIEGO: They are coming closer. I think they will be here any moment now...

NIAR: It doesn't matter. They can't ruin the whole world, can they?

DIEGO: Oh, but it seems that they are definitely trying... They are continuing with what the Europeans started some centuries ago...

NIAR: What if they hit this house, my love?

DIEGO: *(taken aback. Then seriously)*

Well, nothing will really change, right?

BLACKOUT

SCENE FIVE

(The same as Scene 4. One explosion after another; the sounds are becoming louder and louder. Fire behind the window)

DIEGO: *(holding his camera in one hand)*

They are coming.

NIAR: Be they damned... But I can't really hate them. They are just boys; brainwashed, drunk by self-righteousness. They tell them...

(Blast outside)

...They tell them FREEDOM and they repeat it like parrots and go wherever they send them, to spread their dogma like some old crusaders. But freedom is such a complex word. And it means something different for each of us.

DIEGO: I hate them for what they have done to your country.

NIAR: You taught me how to love. I don't want to be burdened by hate. Not now.

(*Another blast breaks windows somewhere nearby. There is a sound of machine gun fire. Short silence, then voices...*)

1st SOLDIER: (*still in the distance*)

Anyone alive..? Get out of your holes, fuckers! Out, shit heads I said!

(*Machinegun fire again*)

DIEGO: (*pulling Niar closer to him*)

Let's stay like this.

NIAR: Don't worry, Diego. They cannot harm me. They cannot do anything to me.

DIEGO: You don't know them...

NIAR: Oh yes, I do. I already had the honor to encounter them once, their precision guided freedom-loving missiles. But now, Diego, they have no power over me. They are no Gods, after all.

DIEGO: What are you saying?

(Door is being kicked from outside)

1st SOLDIER: Open up, assholes!

DIEGO: *(shouts)*

Just calm down, man! I am a Chilean journalist. There is no one here you would be looking for...

1st SOLDIER: *(kicks the door open)*

It's none of your business who I'm looking for, shit-head!

(Diego is still holding Niar. The 1st Soldier comes in, followed by the 2nd soldier. They are looking in the direction of Diego and Niar)

1st SOLDIER: Hi buddy! You look weird. What's wrong with your hands, man?

(Diego releases Niar. His hands fall to his sides. He is still squeezing his camera in the right hand)

2nd SOLDIER: What a stench outside. Seven bodies rotting in the courtyard. I think they'd been there at least two days. Everything is decaying so quickly in this mother-fucking country.

(Niar sits down on the floor, her legs

crossed)

DIEGO: Who are those people outside?

2nd SOLDIER: 'Don't know... probably more collateral damage... the family which used to live here before. Maybe they were trying to escape. Maybe our rookie thought that it was some mother-fucking Muslim military unit in motion... One can't see shit from the air, you know...

1st SOLDIER: Yeah... Fucking right... Muslim military unit my ass...Out of seven, four with tits and headscarves and the rest are children...

2nd SOLDIER: You never know, man. Jihad is jihad, you know...

(He sits on the bed, spreads his legs and scratches his crotch)

Man, my chiefs are all sweaty and itchy in this fucking heat. And we ain't got no fuck'n whores here to scratch them for us...

(Niar gets up, walks to the window, looks outside)

1st SOLDIER: How did you survive here, all alone?

DIEGO: Just luck. And some water that I found...

1st SOLDIER: Now come, you need a medical check-up. By the way, where is that Chile? Chile you said, right? That's next to the United fucking Emirates or stuff, right? Hadn't a clue that you guys look almost like us.

NIAR: *(She turns her face from the window. Facing Diego)*

Go.

(Diego makes an attempt to say something, but she interrupts him)

Go, Diego. Go my love. Go now, and if you really, really want to see me again, I will come. Don't worry. I will come to you.

1st SOLDIER: *(speaking to his friend)*

He's got a really fucked up look on his face. It looks as if he's listening to somebody we can't see. It's kind of spooky. Can you imagine having to live here all by yourself for two days, with all that shelling and corpses behind the window?

DIEGO: *(suddenly screams at both of them)*

Don't you know my country?!

(Both soldiers are looking at him, taken

aback)

Don't you remember? Chile. Try to recall the name. September 11, 1973! You also said that you were defending freedom and democracy then, like here, like now...

2nd SOLDIER: Don't really remember, man. Were you like... you know... also shagged up to the ass by some mother-fucking Muslim fundamentalists or stuff?

DIEGO: No... We had an old president with the thick-framed glasses... And a few poets who believed that there should be a social justice in Chile and all over the world; and we had some bards; some singers... some dreamers. And the world had been listening to us. But that was too much to bear for your country...Too much to bear that we wanted to be free in our own way and not in the way that you push down the throat of the whole world...

(Diego comes to the First Soldier and grabs his shoulders)

...And I had a family like everyone else, a father, a mother, an elder brother. I was going to school in the city of Valparaiso...

1st SOLDIER: *(thoroughly confused)*

So what, buddy? Sounds like things were quite fucking good, right? Sounds like a cool place to grow up. Sounds like fuck'n Canada or something...

NIAR: Diego, don't complicate things. They don't understand; they don't know what you're talking about. They were not told...They just know how to follow the orders... From where I am, it all looks so absurd, so pointless...

DIEGO: *(releases the First Soldier, looking around)*

But where are you, Niar?

NIAR: I am in your heart. I am inside you.

2nd SOLDIER: Who's Niar?

1st SOLDIER: *(whispers)*

Maybe she was his girlfriend or stuff like that. Look, I told you he's not really together... I have no idea what he is talking about. His freedom, our freedom... You know, fuck freedom anyway... Let's go, let's take him to the hospital... It's all very spooky, like some horror movie...

2nd SOLDIER: Mr. Chilean reporter... We are leaving. Please, come with us. You can't stay here. Let's go. We just liberated your ass; we liberated this entire fucking village or whatever it is...

1st SOLDIER: ...regional capital...

2nd SOLDIER: Right... We liberated this entire regional capital and it's time to get the fuck out of here.

1st SOLDIER: Nobody really left to be liberated, man... But still, the effort is what counts, right?!

(1st Soldier lifts up the palm of his right hand and the 2nd Soldier gives him "five")

2nd SOLDIER: That's the spirit!

(Both soldiers are slowly walking towards the door. Diego is following them, walking backwards, looking at Niar)

NIAR: Go! Don't stare at me as if we were parting. Yes, I know... I know, me too, very much. But now, turn around.

(He turns around)

And go...

(Soldiers and Diego leave, closing the door behind them)

Go now...

(Niar is exhausted. She sits down on the floor and she speaks. First with a detached voice but, as the monologue continues, her

voice warms up)

...He insisted on taking me to the Fire Land – to "Tierra de Fuego". It was such a long flight. Before, I was convinced that Buenos Aires was at the end of the world... But we flew two and a half hours straight south – to the town called El Calafate – to the land of glaciers and crystal clear lakes. But even then it was not the end of the world. The plane took off and again still heading south. I was looking through the window all the time; there were no clouds. I saw tremendous rivers and bays, tall mountains, all covered by shining ice and snow. The whole world became white. I couldn't find words to describe the landscape. I imagine that this is how the earth used to be, millions of years ago. I held his hand. Inside me I thanked him for giving me this world, for this great and unexpected gift. The runway was right on the shore of a great river. We landed in Argentina, but on the other side, further south, was Chile again. The airport of Ushuaia was cozy, warm; almost everything was made of wood. We drank cappuccino and took the taxi to the city which was lost under the snow, its streets clean and reassuring. We went to our hotel; stood by the wide window of our room, looking at the enormous bay disappearing from sight with the last rays of the sunlight. It was so cold and windy outside and so warm and comfortable in our room. It was getting dark but we kept looking at this last stretch of land on earth, in silence. Before I met Diego, before my journeys with him, I never left the tropics. I never saw the snow before. I only read about it in books and saw it in films. This was my first snow, the whole world covered by it. The most beautiful snow on earth, he said; the purest. And this was my first love. I never loved before, but as with the snow, I read about it and saw films about it, but never really experienced the taste of it. When it arrived, it was endless. That night when I saw him on the floor of the hotel in my city, bleeding, I knew that I would not be able to abandon him. Before the hotel was bombed, we spoke for two days, unable to part. I didn't want him to leave my town, ever. Or if he had to leave, I wanted to go with him. The explosion came unexpectedly; it ripped my body apart. I was just about to leave... Ready to cross to the other side... Some people would say that I was already dead. But looking at him, I wasn't able to go. I just couldn't. And so I stayed somewhere in between; not here, not there. These things don't happen very often, I suppose, but they happen...

(Niar hears something behind the window. She gets up)

Yes, I will... I will. I am coming now.

BLACKOUT

And

CURTAIN

Andre Vltchek

Plays

Andre Vltchek

ACT TWO

Andre Vltchek

SCENE SIX

There is no intermission between two acts. However, there is a pause that lasts for three minutes. During that time, there is a song of Mercedes Sosa called "Alfonsina y el Mar" playing. The curtain slowly opens during the high pitch piano solo, but the action in Scene 6 doesn't start before the song is almost completely over.

The same settings, the same bar as in the Scene 2.
As "Alfonsina y el Mar" fades away, a low key tango replaces it. Diego is sitting at the table, alone. One couple is sitting not far from him. The waiter slowly approaches his table.

DIEGO: White wine with cherimoya juice, please. And some clams.

WAITER: Yes... immediately.

(Waiter ready to depart, but Diego stops him)

DIEGO: I am back.

WAITER: So it appears. Since you came back from France ten years ago, I can never figure out where you really live. You come and go. You disappear and reappear.

So how was it? There...

DIEGO: *(shrugs his shoulders)*

The same as always... People got killed. Tens of thousands of civilians, innocent men, women, children...

WAITER: Yes, as always, then...

DIEGO: Except that this time it's not over. They are fighting for each village, for each street, for each house... It's a bloodbath...

WAITER: Why did you come back?

DIEGO: I couldn't bear it, anymore. This time I just couldn't bear it. Something happened and I had to leave. I guess that if I'd stayed, I wouldn't be able to be impartial, anymore. I would have had to take sides. I would have had to fight. I wouldn't be able to just report on events...

WAITER: Why didn't you fight, then?

DIEGO: (*taken aback, almost talking to himself*)

One has to fight for somebody. Otherwise it doesn't make much sense, does it? And there was nobody left to fight for...

WAITER: There still are millions of people there...

DIEGO: Yes, but it doesn't work like that. One doesn't fight thinking about millions of abstract people, unfortunately.

WAITER: You look tired and confused. You look angry. It doesn't look like the war is over for you.

DIEGO: It cannot be over. It shouldn't be over, for anybody. Millions of civilians are fighting with their bare hands against the most potent and sophisticated military force on earth. Just to protect their country against invasion. They do it because they can't imagine living under occupation.

WAITER: This war is going to bring the whole world to chaos. Maybe it was one too many.

DIEGO: Maybe.

Suddenly rests his forehead on his palms, changing the subject

Why is it, Enrique, that when we are away, we are dying to return to this city. We talk to strangers about it, we dream about every little street, every corner. But when we come back... it feels and looks like...

WAITER: Like shit?

DIEGO: Exactly.

WAITER: (*The waiter goes away just for a few seconds and comes back with a glass full of white liquid. He touches the back of empty chair*)

May I?

DIEGO: Yes, of course.

WAITER: (*sits down, opposite Diego*)

As you probably know, I used to be a sailor. I used to go all around the world, as many people of Valparaiso still do. I saw the Philippines, Indonesia, China, Germany, Italy, France, South Africa and Canada. I admired ancient cities and ports, bays and tropical beaches. I heard great music from other, distant shores. I ate delicious food, met people of different colors and races. Several times I thought that I had found a paradise. But I always felt the desire to come back to this city – to Valparaiso.

DIEGO: But why, Enrique, why? It's so gloomy and so decayed, its streets are full of potholes. The city is falling apart. Its legends are scary, and sometimes I don't even know who is still alive and who is dead. Its old cable-cars seem to go straight to hell instead of heaven. It rains here, and when it rains the whole world becomes gloomy and gray and there are landslides at the top of the hills, in the poorest parts of the city. When we drink here, we drink until we fall. When we sing, we sometimes howl from desperation.

WAITER: There is no simple answer to your question. It's our home. It's where my home is. And I think your home, too...

DIEGO: Home...

WAITER: And even when you say that you hate Valparaiso, I still feel so much love behind your words...

DIEGO: Maybe... I don't know. I feel that I don't know where my home is, anymore. Maybe it's here, maybe it's in France where I spent so many years in exile, before coming back to Valparaiso. Maybe my home is far away from here, in a beautiful green town on the sea shore of a tropical island in Asia. But that town doesn't exist, anymore. It was destroyed, erased from the map...

(Again, old bolero "Encadenados" playing very softly)

I feel tired.

WAITER: And alone... lonely?

DIEGO: Maybe.

WAITER: You feel like you betrayed someone?

DIEGO: *(looks at the waiter, surprised)*

We are always betraying somebody; it's how things are in this world.

WAITER: All this because she is not with you...

DIEGO: *(His body jerks violently. He grabs the waiter by his hand, looking at him in horror)*

What did you say?! What?!

WAITER: Calm down, man...

DIEGO: How do you know about her?

WAITER: But... you were both here...

DIEGO: *(forcefully)*

No! No. What are you talking about?

(*He gets up, gets behind his chair, holding back of it*)

It was just a dream, Enrique. She was not here; in Valparaiso, her body was rotting under the concrete beams. She was buried alive after an American missile hit her hotel. We talked for two days before... But I never saw her after the blast. How could I? She was dead. She is dead! Dead! She was killed and I was injured. And someone took me to her house simply because it was one of the very few houses that were still standing. In front of her house, there were seven bodies – the bodies of her family - rotting in the tropical heat. Someone put me to bed; I have no idea who was it. The rest was just my fantasy, the result of my fever, my injuries. I was asleep; probably dying, unconscious...

WAITER: You drank wine. She drank cherimoya juice, with ice. She had a beautiful serene face. Her head was covered. There was one pearl on the top of her scarf.

DIEGO: (*sits down*)

Shut up! Stop.

WAITER: The same bolero. The same table... Her name is...

DIEGO: Stop I am begging you!

WAITER: ...Niar.

DIEGO: (*breaks down, his forehead hits the table*)

I am damned.

WAITER: She spoke to you at the reception of her hotel where you were staying. She developed certain feelings for you. Then the hotel was hit by the American missile. She... Well, you were hit, injured. She refused to go. She carried you home...

DIEGO: What are you telling me? Refused to go? Since when is it our choice whether to stay or to go?

WAITER: (*making a face, almost mocking Diego*)

Sometimes it is. She couldn't let you stay where you were, injured and unconscious... and alone. Or could she?

DIEGO: That's insane!

WAITER: (*suddenly transforms himself from somewhat mysterious creature to what he really is: a good natured and simple waiter from the port of Valparaiso*)

Fuck, Diego!

(He downs Diego's glass of wine in one gulp)

So who said that love should be sane?

DIEGO: Who told you all this?

WAITER: She did of course. We became quite good friends, while you were hanging around the world, licking your wounds before coming back home...

DIEGO: Niar? She told you all this?

(There is a long sound of a ship's siren coming from outside; from the port. A woman appears on the stage. She is around forty, elegant and alone. The music changes, it becomes very low-key, the piano is playing the theme-song from Saura's "Cria Cuervas". The woman slowly dances. Soft light is reflected in a kitchy crystal ball hanging from the ceiling. The light is bluish. All other lights gradually off)

Who is she?

WAITER: *(this time he is surprised)*

You can see her?

DIEGO: Of course I can.

WAITER: Good. She is... well; a woman...

DIEGO: That much I already understood...

WAITER: My woman...

DIEGO: I didn't know that you...

WAITER: Well, nobody really knows...

(They are both mesmerized, looking at her dancing)

DIEGO: I never met her before. Who is she, really?

WAITER: Does it matter?

(The other couple continues talking; ignoring the appearance of LAURA. It is obvious that they cannot see her)

DIEGO: She is beautiful.

WAITER: *(Mocking Diego)*

What a good taste you have, my friend. I knew her for twenty years. For me, she is the most beautiful woman on earth. We met in Barcelona, the city where my ship called in one day. We spent one week together. Then I left, I had to leave; I had to sail back. Then certain things happened...

DIEGO: Certain things?

(Diego goes away. Soon he comes back

with a full, uncorked bottle of red wine and two glasses)

WAITER: Yes, certain things. Her life was unbearable, for many different reasons.

DIEGO: And?

WAITER: She ended it. Then she came here.

DIEGO: To you?

WAITER: Yes. Back in Barcelona I told her all about Valparaiso. I told her how far it was; you see she wanted to go very far away... I also told her that I would be waiting for her. I told her about the streets climbing the hills and about the rain, about the colorful metal sheets covering the houses from humidity and the brutal stormy winds coming from the ocean, about the enormous ships that ran ashore and now are rotting like ghosts on the coasts of Valparaiso and Vina del Mar. We spoke the whole night together, before my ship had to sail away, back to Chile. And one day she came. She used to be much older than me. Now she is younger.

DIEGO: You never married, Enrique...

WAITER: No, not in a church, not at the city hall, not the way it is usually done. But she is...

DIEGO: What is her name?

WAITER: Laura.

(*The music is becoming more and more muted; some lights come back but the stage is still in semi-darkness. Then the music stops, but the woman is still center stage, slowly moving. Then suddenly, drops of rain hit the metal roof. It is a very loud sound followed by the howling of the wind. A man walks in, huaso-style hat, long raincoat; he is wet. He sits at one of the tables, showing his back, face invisible. Laura sits next to him. They talk but their voices are not audible*)

DIEGO: (*suddenly calm*)

It feels so good here.

WAITER: Yes. Niar likes it here, too. She comes almost every evening. She doesn't cover her head anymore. She reads books and is learning Spanish. I am helping her. I got her hooked on Le Monde Diplomatique; she uses her dictionary to read it. She even learned some local slang. Cherimoya is still her favorite juice. She's developed a taste for olives.

DIEGO: They can't see them, can they? Other people, I mean.

WAITER: Not necessarily. Some can see them, some can't. There are no set rules, you know. They themselves determine by whom they want to be seen. One little luxury that you and I don't have...

DIEGO: When we were taking our trips together... back then... she never spoke about her family. They were all killed in front of her house. Does she ever speak to you about them?

WAITER: No. As far as she is concerned, she never lost them. She is in between, not here and not there. She is in touch with them as she is in touch with us. The worst thing about other people's dying is a loss of our ability to communicate with them. She never lost that ability - that's why she is not grieving for them.

DIEGO: (*filling the glass of wine and downing it in one gulp. Suddenly smiling at the waiter*)

So ghosts do exist, after all, Enrique!

WAITER: Well, call it whatever you want...

(*A man sitting at one of the tables gets up and walks towards the big, bulky old fashioned radio. He turns the knob, then a loud pre-recorded broadcast*)

RADIO: (*woman's voice*) It is 5 o'clock in the afternoon and you are listening to the news bulletin of the broadcasting service of

Chile Dos.

(Strong static, nothing could be heard for several seconds. Then:)

...hit the capital city. Among the casualties were several international relief workers. The sky is covered by a thick cloud of smoke, coming from burning buildings. Tens of thousands of civilians are trying to escape, carrying their most essential belongings with them. There are corpses lining all the main highways and access roads. Local and foreign doctors are working without rest, overwhelmed by the constant influx of casualties. All medical posts ran out of medicine and anesthetics several days ago. There is heavy fighting on the outskirts of the capital. American, British and Australian forces have to fight for every house and every street. Carpet bombing of the suburbs continues around the clock. The estimated death toll amongst civilians in the capital city alone is now 40 thousand.

The European Union, at its extraordinary session in Brussels, refused to endorse the military action. However, while critical of the invasion itself, the French President and German Chancellor emphasized the importance of the trans-Atlantic relationship. They called on the United Nations to immediately move its troops to the country once fighting ends.

There were large peaceful anti-war demonstrations in almost all European capitals. After giving several speeches and marching in an orderly fashion through the city centers, the demonstrators returned to their homes. There were no reported confrontations with the police and no arrests.

Students in several South American cities clashed with the police. Zokalo - main square of Mexico City - is still occupied by protesting members of PRD, trade unions and students.

The governments of Brazil, Venezuela and Argentina strongly condemned the American led invasion.

Malaysia declared a state of emergency shortly after midnight and its Prime Minister stated that his country may not be able to stay away for long from the conflict while the neighboring nation is being devastated by foreign troops.

Chile: Riots erupted in two port cities: Antofagasta and Valparaiso. Protesters are demanding the end of impunity for the Chilean military and for several ruling families responsible for the 1973 coup. They are also demanding the end of the war in Asia. There are calls for the government to immediately break all diplomatic relations with the United States, the United Kingdom and Australia...

(A man turns off the radio. Silence for several seconds)

(A woman enters. Her long, black hair is wet. She comes straight to the table, pats the waiter on the back, than embraces Diego with all her strength. Diego stands up. She kisses his face, his hands, than throws her arms around his neck)

DIEGO: *(thoroughly confused, terrified and in the same time excited)*

Mother...

MOTHER: *(detaches herself from him. Then she smiles)*

Enrique, bring me a big glass of white wine, will you?

WAITER: Immediately.

(The waiter leaves but soon comes back with a big glass full of white wine)

MOTHER: *(to Diego)*

You look so worried, my love...

(She extends her hand, touching his hair, gently)

DIEGO: *(slowly regaining his ability to*

speak)

Exactly thirty years, mother. I haven't seen you for thirty years. Now you look much younger than me...

(He embraces her, first hesitantly, than with the full force)

MOTHER: But I was watching over every step of yours. I never left you, Diego. Your father and I never left you.

DIEGO: You never...?

FATHER: *(Father, a man who was sitting with the huaso- hat at the table now standing and coming slowly to the table)*

Too much unfinished business left on this earth, my boy. We couldn't leave just like that. And you were also here, alone...

(Diego backs up, hits his back against the wall, covers his face with the palm of his hand, then again looks at his parents)

DIEGO: You are both here.

FATHER: Yes, and we will all go home now.

(They come together, forming a small circle in the middle of the stage, pressing their heads together as they stand. There is

tremendous pain but also relief in their posture. They don't move for several seconds. Then:)

BLACKOUT

SCENE SEVEN

A dining room in an old house of Valparaiso, a long table and several seats, two chairs at the wall and one painting.

The sound of wind and rain at the beginning of the scene, then gradually all sounds disappear.

Niar enters the room, very neatly dressed. She sits down on one of the chairs, opens a book and starts reading.

Diego and his father and mother enter shortly after. Their overcoats are wet. They are cheerful.

Niar gets up abruptly, runs towards them and embraces Diego. Both mother and father greet her by touching her hands and shoulders.

DIEGO: I was such a fool. I was refusing to believe it until now... until I saw you...

NIAR: But I promised...

DIEGO: Forgive me. My faith...

NIAR: You didn't trust me.

DIEGO: I never learned how to trust. For my entire life I was taught how not to trust anybody and anything. I had never any faith in religions, in all those words being constantly uttered by our rulers, no faith in the media...

FATHER: (*laughing*)

That's why you are a journalist... a writer.

DIEGO: (*confused*)

I never lost faith in the language, in words, in the ability of words to express facts and innermost feelings. But I have no faith left for those who now use those words...

MOTHER: Until you met Niar.

DIEGO: Yes, until I met her.

FATHER: Now come, all of you. Let's sit at the table. Let's be together, we are a family.

(They all sit down at the table)

Niar lives with us, Diego. She became... like our own daughter. We did everything possible to make her feel comfortable here, with us. She has a Muslim background and your mother and I were always Marxists. We don't know much about religions, but we tried... you know, we tried to talk. And we talked for many nights and we came to some conclusions.

DIEGO: What sort of conclusions?

NIAR: Well, for instance that people shouldn't be left starving when there is plenty of food around. That people shouldn't be allowed to die when there is plenty of medicine that can cure them...

MOTHER: We tried to understand each other. And we did, at the end.

DIEGO:

(Stands up, starts pacing up and down the room, worried)

But what will happen now? How long can you...

(He doesn't finish his sentence)

FATHER: How long are we going to stay?

DIEGO: *(With difficulty)*

Yes.

FATHER: Everything will probably change tonight, Diego.

DIEGO: Tonight?!

MOTHER: Don't be scared, my child. Everything will change for the better.

DIEGO: *(Confused, frightened)*

But how can anything change for the better? Now when you are all back... This is the first time that I feel I am really living...

FATHER: *(Laughing)*

Yes, we may be dead, but we are still much more alive then most of them... outside. More alive than those poor slaves and robots petrified by their mortgages, strangled by the jobs they hate...

MOTHER: *(Mockingly)*

Would you please stop your speeches, dear?

FATHER: I apologize.

DIEGO: *(Doesn't really follow the conversation)*

You are still a big man, father, as big as I always remembered you. They took you away when I was still a child, in the middle of the night. And as they were taking you away, I watched from the widow, I saw how you walked, so proud, so erect; they had to keep pace with you, those cowards. You and the soldiers were walking down the street of Cerro Allegre, towards their black car. I never saw you again, but I heard that no matter what they did to you later, you never betrayed anybody; they never could make you do anything against your conscience and against your people. And I was so proud of you, father; all those years. I always thought: "What would he think if he could see me now..."

FATHER: You did well, my boy. And by the way, I was always there, you know... almost always... I was there when you were smuggled by comrades across the border to Peru, I was there when your grandmother flew to South America, to Lima, searching for you, finding you. I was there when she tried to explain why you had to go to France with her. You enjoyed your first flight, but right after you arrived, a couple of days later, you were searching for the port in Paris, for big ships and cranes. You didn't understand why there is no sea.

MOTHER: *(Laughs at him)*

We were there, you pompous old man, not just you.

FATHER: Yes, *we* were there. And we were there, that day, when the hotel was hit.

NIAR: It wasn't just me who carried you to my house, Diego. All three of us were... I met them; your parents at that moment when I decided not to leave you.

FATHER: And then we took Niar to Valparaiso, to the city of your childhood, of our youth, of our victories!

MOTHER: *(Mockingly)*

Oh god, again! Do we have to salute now?

DIEGO: But how many of you live here, in Valparaiso?

FATHER: Haven't you ever noticed how many people of this city look as if they live two parallel lives? They walk down the streets, hardly noticing their surroundings. They are here, but also somewhere else. Those people have visitors...

DIEGO: But why? Why are you really here? Why are they here?

MOTHER: We have to defend this world; to defend those who are still alive.

DIEGO: But why here, why in Valparaiso?

FATHER: One has to start somewhere. And don't you know that Valparaiso was always a city of ghosts...

DIEGO: And defend against what; against whom?

FATHER: Against what happened to you, Diego; and against what happened to y... and to your wife; to all of us... and to those who are now throwing stones at tanks, twelve thousand kilometers from here, in Asia.

(Diego and Niar look at each other)

DIEGO: My wife...

(Niar bends her head, avoids his eyes)

NIAR: You asked me once...

DIEGO: Yes I did. Yes, you are my wife. Yes, I never loved any other woman as much as I love you.

(Suddenly desperate, he throws himself on top of the table, holding the edges, screams...)

But you are dead! You are all dead!! Dead!!!

MOTHER: *(Comes to him, slowly, puts her*

hand gently on his head, strokes his hair)

My silly boy... My little silly boy...

(Diego is shaking under her touch)

DIEGO: Mother...

NIAR: *(Gets up, joins mother, caresses Diego's shoulders. Very quietly, tenderly)*

We didn't choose to die, my love. I thought, I hoped that our love could make my death irrelevant...

DIEGO: But it is relevant! I want to have a child with you. I want the whole world to see us together, walking down the street... I want you to age with me...

NIAR: *(Slowly)*

That... may not be possible.

(Diego, suddenly horrified by his own words)

DIEGO: I am sorry... I am so sorry...

(The lights get suddenly dimmer. Mother slowly withdraws her hand. Niar covers her mouth with the palm of her hand)

Wait...

(Lights even dimmer)

Wait! You want to go, don't you? Why? Why do you want to go? You knew it... You told me everything will change, tonight! I don't want anything to change. I am scared. This is the first time in my entire life that I have a family. I have all three of you; it's all I need. Nothing else, I swear. Only you! Please don't abandon me now. My entire life I have been living in solitude!

FATHER: There are certain rules...

MOTHER: Some spells...

NIAR: Even in the other world.

FATHER: We may have to go now.

DIEGO: *(Screams)*

Stay! Or I will follow you.

NIAR: *(In a very strong, determined voice)*

No!

DIEGO: There's nothing here; on this side. Just plunder and lies, just money and greed, misery, slavery and cowardice! You forget that this is not the same world anymore. It all changed. It's cold here. There is no god, no revolution, there is nothing sacred left;

there are hardly any dreams, any desires on this earth. There is nothing left if you go. Nothing!

NIAR: There is. And you will live your life to the fullest, for me and for them; for all of us.

FATHER: And you will fight for all of us, and for those who are still alive.

MATHER: And we will always be near you...

NIAR: There is also my country, don't you forget. I gave it to you that day, my first day in Valparaiso and it's yours now; with all its silence and the immensity of its seas, with its music and tenderness and beauty. It's bleeding now; don't abandon it... And I will come to you again, Diego. I will come very soon, if you really want me to. I promised before and I kept my word. I am giving you my promise again. I swear. But remember, when I come back, I may have a different face, but it will be me and when you see me, you will recognize me.

DIEGO: (*Bitterly*)

You never even taught me how to pray...

NIAR: Do you want to pray?

DIEGO: No. I just wanted to know how it

feels, how you feel when you...

NIAR: Don't pray Diego... Live!

MOTHER: Goodbye, Diego, my son. Be as brave and kind as you were until now. We are always with you.

FATHER: We have to go.

DIEGO: But I love you! I love all of you...

FATHER: We love you, too. I'll be damned if we don't.

DIEGO: Wait!

FATHER: Tonight, Diego, is your night. Many things will be decided... tonight. Be... hell, just be what you are!

(Father, Mother and Niar are slowly approaching each other. They embrace briefly, as if seeking support from each other. Then they walk towards the door, slowly. One single light illuminates the door. It is open, Laura is waiting. She joins three of them. They exit. Diego is standing in the middle of the room, holding his head between both hands, staring at the space in horror)

BLACKOUT

Andre Vltchek

SCENE EIGHT

The same bar as in the Scene 6. Diego and the waiter are sitting at the table, talking. Nobody else, except one man with his back to the stage.
The scene opens with a woman singing "Valparaiso" of Gitano Rodriguez:

"Yo no he sabido de su historia,
un dia naci alli, sencillamenete.
el viejo puerto vigilo mi infancia
con rostro de fria indiferencia.

porque no naci pobre y siempre tuve
un miedo inconcebible a la pobreza.
yo les quiero contra lo que he observado
para que nos vayamos conociendo.

el habitante encadeno las calles
la lluvia destino las escaleras
y un manto de tristeza fue cubriendo

los ceros con sus calles y sus ninos

*Y vino el temporal y la llovizna
con su carga de arena y desperdicio.*

*Ppor ahi paso la muerte tantas veces
la muerte que enluto a Valparaiso
y una vez mas el viento como siempre
limpio la cara de este puerto herido.*

*Pero este Puerto amarra como el hambre,
no se puede vivir sin conocerlo,
no se puede mirar sin que nos falte,
la brea, el viento sur, los volantines,
el pescador de jaivas que entristecen
nuestro paisaje de la costanera.*

Yo no sabia nunca de su historia..."

DIEGO: I killed them the second time.

WAITER: No, in a way you released them. And anyway, you didn't know. You broke the spell, but you knew nothing about it...

DIEGO: Everything seems so meaningless now.

WAITER: It will all sort itself out very soon.

DIEGO: You too are saying this? What do you know? What will sort itself out? And why are you so calm? Laura left, too didn't she?

WAITER: Yes, but I don't think that we saw the end of it all.

(A man stands up and walks heavily towards their table. He is drunk, his hair is in disorder)

1st SOLDIER: Diego.

DIEGO: Who are you? Do we know each other?

1st SOLDIER: I am sorry.

DIEGO: But who are you?

1st SOLDIER: *(Screams)*

I am sorry!

DIEGO: Damn, you will make me deaf! Yes, I know you. What on earth brings you here?

1st SOLDIER: The house where we found you... the field hospital. I came to visit you several times, we talked for many hours...

DIEGO: Yes. What are you doing here?

1st SOLDIER: Shortly after you left I was injured, then discharged from the army. Back there you told me that if I ever wanted to find you, I could come to Valparaiso, to this bar. I wandered allover Asia... for several weeks, I talked to people... then I decided to come.

DIEGO: What did they tell you..? What did the people of Asia tell you?

1st SOLDIER: Similar things that you told me in the hospital. We fucked up, man. We fucked up no end and we didn't even know it. I kept thinking about your family, about Chile... I knew nothing about Chile before meeting you. In Asia I met men and women who were willing to talk to me despite the war, to share their meal, to listen...I felt so ashamed. I never saw them before as...

DIEGO: As human beings?

1st SOLDIER: Exactly... Before I saw them just as our enemies; they were fanatics living in their weird universe. That's what I was taught. I was told that we had to liberate them, save them from themselves, save ourselves from them. Man, but I learned that we had been continuously shagging them for long centuries...

DIEGO: Who did?

1st SOLDIER: We... The whites: the Europeans and now us – the Americans.

WAITER: (*Ironically but in a friendly way*)

Have something stronger. I will bring you some pisco, it's on the house. We have to drink to that revelation...

(He leaves but soon returns with a bottle full of yellowish liquid, fills a small glass and hands it over to the 1st Soldier).

1st SOLDIER: *(He is holding the shot glass in his hand then downs it in the middle of the following monologue)*

And all they really want is to live their own life, right...? live their way. But we never let them. We forced our economic system on them and if they didn't want it, we bribed their elites or simply bought them, so that they could shag their own people on our behalf. And if even that didn't work, we just went in; we supported the coups, we killed their presidents and if that wasn't enough, we invaded the place altogether. And we always had some lofty pretext handy. We fucked up, man...

WAITER: So what will you do now, soldier?

1st SOLDIER: I don't know. He...

(He nods towards Diego)

... He is my friend. He was the first person who was willing to talk to me about all this. So I came here solely to ask him this question: What can be done, what can I do?

DIEGO: I don't know myself.

1st SOLDIERE: (*Distressed*)

But you have to know. What do you mean by "I don't know"? You understand this world. Thanks to you, I am starting to understand it, too... You have to tell me... There has to be some solution.

DIEGO: They told you before what to do, and you were doing it, right?

1st SOLDIER: Right...

DIEGO: But they were wrong. You were made to kill innocent people as a result...

1st SOLDIER: That's true...

DIEGO: But now... How do you know that I have the right answers... why do you always have to rely on somebody else?

1st SOLDIER: Because I know so little, because most of us know next to nothing. You know much more, you have to have some answers...

DIEGO: But I don't want to tell anybody what to do. I am lost myself...

WAITER: (*Smiling*)

That won't do, Diego...

DIEGO: So what should I say? Should I tell him he should fight? Should I tell him he should fight fascism? Nobody can fight it, anymore... It's too late; it's spread like a cancer. It is in charge of everything, from media to schools, from economy to politics... from supermarket to people's bedrooms... they watch it, inhale it, shit it, shop for it, they were taught how to admire it, how not to be able to even imagine their lives without it... everywhere in the world...

1st SOLDIER: I asked around Valparaiso about your father. He was an important man before 1973, wasn't he? They all told me that he was a great man and even those who disagreed with him kept repeating it. Then, after the coup, he was arrested. They tortured him for three weeks, crushed his balls and broke his legs. But he was still screaming insults to their faces. And then they threw him into the sea. They raped your mother and cut off her breasts; loaded her into a military helicopter, cut her belly open, tied her hands behind her back and threw her into the Pacific Ocean. They shot your brother like a dog, at the side of the road. And my government knew all about this, it was paying for it, it was helping to plan all those massacres. Don't you feel mad, Diego? Don't you want to fight?

DIEGO: *(Suddenly exhausted)*

I am not sure that I want to fight. And I am

not sure that I want to live. There are limits to everything. I covered wars for fifteen years. You saw one war, I saw dozens of them. You were behind your machine gun, most of the time inside your armored vehicle. I had to get very close; I had to get right next to the people who were still bleeding, dying in some gutter or under the rubble of their collapsed houses. I had to witness the mess left by your smart bombs, your cluster bombs, your precision guided missiles; your freedom loving missions that were flattening schools and hospitals, press offices and food depots...

1st SOLDIER: (*Desperate*)

I said I'm sorry, man! If I'd refused to go, they would've locked me up...

DIEGO: It's not about you being sorry. Do you think I am blaming you? Do you think I would be different if I grew up in the same place as you? Well, maybe I would be, but I am not so sure.

(*1st Soldier is looking down on the table in front of him*)

I saw so much misery in this world that you can hardly imagine it. I wrote about it, the best I could. Now I just want to be left alone...

1st SOLDIER: So all this madness will go on? So there is no more hope for the rest of the world? So these few rich bandit states can continue spreading their power all over the globe? You opened my eyes, how can you now back out?

DIEGO: I only told you the truth about the past. I never offered any coherent vision for the future.

WAITER: *(shakes his head)*

No, that will not do Diego... That will not do...

1st SOLDIER: So everything is lost, then? There is no way to correct wrongs, no way to reverse the path of the history?

DIEGO: I don't know.

1st SOLDIER: Then what's the point of knowing? What's the point of realizing all this and then landing on some comfortable sofa and doing nothing?

DIEGO: *(Speaks heavily)*

In one day, in one single day I gained everything and then I lost it all. I feel empty and exhausted. This city played some tricks on me. I can hardly distinguish between the real and the imaginary world. I don't know when I am asleep and when I am awake. Those who had once been dead were just talking to me; they offered their love. Then they left, without even a proper goodbye.

WAITER: *(Appalled)*

Stop being sorry for yourself, Diego! You are your father's son. You can't just whine... You can lead.

DIEGO: But I don't want to lead! Don't you understand that all I want right now is to have a home; a family, a place where I can return night after night? I've been living with my memories, with ghosts since the coup of 73! And the only woman I ever truly loved turned out to be similar to everything else in my past; an unreal being and as imaginary as everything else... I need something now, something real, something that will not go away tomorrow, something I can cling to, physically, every evening, every night and then every morning.

(To the soldier)

Don't you understand why they are fighting for every house there, where you just came from? Because they have those physical ties; they have something to defend, something to fight for! They are not fighting for some lofty ideas, they are fighting for human lives, for their wives and children, for their streets and houses, for their country, its beaches and rivers, its forests, for their language, their stones, their sand, their flowers, their trees...

1st SOLDIER (*Suddenly determined*)

You won't discourage me. I helped to destroy their world. If I cannot find anything of my own worth fighting for, I will fight for their world, then. I owe it to them... to those people I bombed for weeks and months.

WAITER: That is... quite noble.

DIEGO: You've found your answer, then. You found it yourself. You don't need me to tell you what to do.

1st SOLDIER: I needed to see you and to talk to you; I needed to understand your story. I had to see the city of Valparaiso.

DIEGO: You've seen it. You've seen me. You've heard my story, soldier. I am burned, empty and useless. And now you know it.

1st SOLDIER: Now I know the story. And I see you are suffering from some tremendous loss. But I know your type – I saw people like you before the battle: you will be strong again, in no time. You will fight. I swear you will.

(*Long howl of the siren coming from the port and cry of the seagulls. Then:*)

BLACKOUT

Andre Vltchek

SCENE NINE

The same as Scene 8. Diego, Waiter and 1st Soldier are sitting at the table in the empty bar in Valparaiso. The sound of wind, seagulls and the rain, drumming loudly on the metal roof.

Then the door opens. Two women enter, one is Spanish and one Asian.
Victoria, the Spanish woman, is played by the same actress as Laura.
The Asian woman has long black hair falling on her shoulders. She is dressed elegantly, according to the latest fashion. She is played by the same actress as Niar.
Both women came from outside; from the rain.

SPANISH WOMAN: (*To no one in particular*)

Good evening. We are travelers; we were both caught in the rain, looking for a warm place to rest. We arrived from Santiago this morning... we both fell in love with this city. We walked for several hours through its hills and then we were told that there will be no more buses returning to the capital. The city was in turmoil, there were barricades growing around the Congress... And then the rain began...

ASIAN WOMAN: (*As in case of the Spanish woman, she speaks to no one in particular*)

It was always my dream to visit this part of the world but while I was traveling, my country was invaded by the American army. I come from the capital city, I am a writer. Now my city is in ruins. I have no way to return. I have no news of my family.

WAITER: Welcome. You came to the right place. Take off your coats, I will take them to the kitchen, so they can dry next to the stove.

(*He takes their raincoats and disappears. A few moments later he comes back, holding two cups of tea*).

Drink this, you are wet.

SPANISH WOMAN: Thank you. Like my friend, I always wanted to come to your country, but for many years I felt it was not the right time, yet. Now I feel I am expected here...

WAITER: What is your name?

SPANISH WOMAN: My name is Victoria.

WAITER: (*mesmerized, repeats*)

Victoria...

(*There is a sound of bells coming from outside, then sirens of the ambulance*)

ASIAN WOMAN: (*Comes straight to Diego*)

I was told that I should look for you. I was informed that you just returned from my country. I am all alone; I have no place to go.

DIEGO: (*Suddenly excited*)

Who told you... please tell me...

ASIAN WOMAN: It doesn't matter. I was told that I can trust you... and that you would understand.

DIEGO: (*Gets up, with tremendous care and tenderness leads her to the chair, helping her to sit down*)

Yes of course... I do understand.

(*Puts his hand to the pocket of his*

trousers, taking out a set of keys, handing them to her)

These are the keys to your home. Welcome.

ASIAN WOMAN: *(Taken aback a little bit)*

Pardon me?

DIEGO: Take these keys...

(She hesitantly takes them and puts them to her beg)

Please stay in my house. Don't go away; stay as long as you want. Stay forever. Please do stay forever.

ASIAN WOMAN: But...

DIEGO: *(Looks straight at her)*

There is no need for words...

(She nods and then she smiles, faintly)

(The waiter and Spanish Woman are engaged in conversation on the other side of the table, but their words are not audible. The 1st Soldier is looking at both couples, mesmerized. Then he walks towards the radio, turns up the volume, then lights a cigarette)

VOICE FROM THE RADIO: (*A female voice*)

...desperate resistance. There is no water in the city, and the sewage treatment system has collapsed. American troops made an attempt to break into the center of the capital using armored vehicles and tanks, but after encountering massive resistance withdraw towards the international airport, calling for air support. The suburbs were again savagely bombed. There seems to be no house left intact on the Western outskirts. The situation is that of total chaos and despair. International relief organizations are unable to deliver food and medicine; almost all press agencies evacuated the country after being deliberately targeted by invading troops.

Millions of citizens of two neighboring Asian countries are marching through their capitals, demanding an immediate mobilization of troops and military action in support of their neighbor.

Chile: There are violent clashes of demonstrators with the police in Valparaiso. The government declared a state of emergency two hours ago. All demonstrations are banned throughout the country. After two students died, Valparaiso erupted in spontaneous revolt; there are barricades growing in the downtown area. Tens of thousands of protestors are marching through the Avenida Pedro Montt, carrying banners with Salvador Allende's face, chanting: "No forgiveness, no forgetting!" referring to those responsible for the death of at least four thousand people during and after the military coup of 1973. A huge crowd broke into the house of retired general Antonio Mierdez...

(Short pause)

Son-of-a-bitch; old Nazi fucker...

(Another short pause)

Mierdez is known to be responsible for some of the bloodiest atrocities during the military dictatorship. The situation is tense and explosive. The injured are being taken by ambulance to the hospitals in Valparaiso and Vina del Mar.

(Some sounds, inaudible muted conversations)

Look, I can't do this, anymore... No, shut up, I just can't!

(Pause)

...There are reports just in that two columns of military vehicles left the barracks and moved towards the National Congress. However, our correspondent who is in front of the congress building says that the soldiers refused to open fire on demonstrators. There is a scene of total chaos: soldiers are sitting on top of their vehicles, smoking and talking to protestors. Asked about his behavior, one of the soldiers explained: "As far as I am concerned, my duty and obligation is to protect Chile from external enemies, not to shoot civilians of my own country".

(*Pause*)

Just get up from your sofas and go to the streets. We have suffered; we have lived in lies for long enough! I went to the country they are bombing now... I went there last year, as a tourist. It's the most beautiful country on earth. Let's not allow it to be reduced to rubble. Let's go, everybody! And here, in Chile?! We still have the same hundred mostly Fascist families running the whole country, we still have a German Nazi colony in the south enjoying impunity! Do you really want to live in this kind of world for the rest of your lives?

(*Static, then the broadcast gets interrupted*)

1st SOLDIER: (*Exited*)

It's starting, damn it!

ASIAN WOMAN: (*To Diego*)

I know you... We met before, don't you agree? I don't remember when or where. Today I was rushing to meet you; I felt this path is leading me home. Please forgive me; I never spoke like this before...

DIEGO: Don't apologize. All that is happening is right. Just never leave again.

ASIAN WOMAN: I don't think I can.

(Suddenly the door flies open. The sound of wind and of sirens, the roar of a crowd. Young men and women run inside, holding banners with Allende and Diego's father)

GIRL STUDENT: We are going! We are going up; to the National Congress!

BOY STUDENT: We will take the Congress and try to start everything all over again, where it was destroyed, interrupted thirty years ago!

(Looks at the Asian Woman, taken aback, then with great reverence)

We will do it for your sake, too, sister; for the sake of your land! And we will build a much better world later, all of us, together! Come with us, all of you!

1st SOLDIER: What about me? Can I come, too?

GIRL STUDENT: (*Looks at him, mockingly*)

You are quite a man, gringo! Big and strong and tall; I like that. So you are on our side, too?

(*Swept away by her, nodding stupidly*)

1st SOLDIER: I am with you. Yes.

(*He is looking at her*)

Can I come with *you?*

(*She is still laughing, happily and mockingly*)

GIRL STUDENT: Of course you can; come with me darling gringo.

(*She comes closer and gives him a kiss straight on the lips. He stands up*)

BOY STUDENT: Come all of you! We need every man, every woman. This is just a beginning. Come!

(*Sound of police sirens from the distance. Sounds of the street battle until the end of the play*)

ASIAN WOMAN: (*Stands up, too. Comes very close to Diego*)

Come Diego. I will go with you.

DIEGO: Are you sure you are ready to go? It's getting very dangerous...

ASIAN WOMAN: I trust you. I will not leave your side...

DIEGO: But do you promise that you will hold on to me?

(*In a slow, almost childlike gesture she takes his hand*)

ASIAN WOMAN: I will...

DIEGO: And tonight we will go to my house together. And you will stay until it is safe to go back to your country. And even then you won't go alone; we will return there together.

(*Waiter and Spanish Woman are still deep in conversation. 1st Soldier is talking to the Girl Student*)

(*Suddenly, the Asian Woman speaks. It is obvious it takes her an enormous effort to pronounce these words*)

ASIAN WOMAN: You are not betraying her, Diego. She is inside me; I took her inside me – she had no other place to go. She... passed everything necessary to me. There was no other way. If you accept me, I will stay with you, forever. I am me and her. And from now on, I will be the only woman in your life; I will be your home, your family and your love.

DIEGO: I know. I understood that from the moment you walked in. And I do accept...

ASIAN WOMAN: (*Looking at the distance*)

You took her to Peru, Diego.

DIEGO: I took *you* to Peru.

ASIAN WOMAN: Yes, me!

DIEGO: I took *you* to Peru. I took you to Bolivia and to Peru, to Potosi and Cusco, and to Ayacucho... to the places high in the mountains, in which these horrors we are all now experiencing really started. I showed you the places where human dignity and identity were taken away from the people, together with their religions, culture, languages and architecture. Where the old palaces and temples were destroyed and the stones were used for building Spanish-style cities and cathedrals. I took you up there, to the land where the silent, motionless faces of poor indigenous men, women and children are like an enormous monument to our brutality and terror.

ASIAN WOMAN: And there, on the slopes of Ollantaytambo, you read me another poem by Pablo Neruda...

DIEGO: Yes, "The Heights of MachuPichu"...

ASIAN WOMAN: ...But this time it was not a poem about love, but about the people of this continent uniting, breaking their shackles and going to the final battle against those who were tormenting them for centuries.

(As she speaks, there is the sound of the music from the altiplane. However, the sound of the street battle outside continues to be heard)

DIEGO: It's a poem about regained dignity, about pride and about people's right to defend their lives.

ASIAN WOMAN: Yes, Diego. But it was not the only place you took me to in Peru. First we traveled to a border town between Chile and Peru – to Arica. The desert was immense. They say it's the driest place on earth – the Desert of Atacama. But it's not where you crossed the border when you were a child...

DIEGO: No, we went straight to the mountains, towards Bolivia. We had to hide. The entire area was controlled by the military. We slept one night in the house of indigenous people; we slept in the hut on the mud floor. I had mountain sickness, I had a headache, and was vomiting the whole night.

ASIAN WOMAN: You took me there, too. They are still alive; that family that gave you and your guides shelter thirty years ago. In the morning your two guides finally told you what happened to your family.

DIEGO: They did; they had to. I understood nothing then.

ASIAN WOMAN: You didn't know what to say. And you looked around and there were just these bare, gray mountains growing from the desert. I never saw such a lonely, desolate place, anywhere on earth.

DIEGO: Yes, we were in the desert, but it was still so cold in the morning. They covered my shoulders with a colorful poncho. They put a hot cup of tea into my hands, but I was still shaking.

ASIAN WOMAN: When they finally told you... you didn't cry, did you?

DIEGO: No, there were no tears coming from my eyes. I felt ashamed, I thought that I was obliged to cry, I even tried, but there were no tears coming from my eyes. I felt they were still there, with me... my parents.

ASIAN WOMAN: How old were you?

DIEGO: I was eleven years old.

ASIAN WOMAN: What did you feel? Tell me, because this may be waiting for me very soon, when we go home. Or sooner... so please, tell me the truth.

DIEGO: It's different. You have me. We will cry together, I won't leave you for one single moment. But back there, I had nobody. There was a condor flying high in the sky, almost touching the first peaks of the Andes. There were two friends of my parents with me; guides who were helping me to cross the border to Peru, but I had never met them before... to me they were strangers. After they spoke... it was as if all sounds had disappeared. There were no sounds and no colors, just deadly silence and an indifferent wind caressing the smooth surface of the desert. I felt that I would suffocate, I felt pain in my chest, couldn't speak.

ASIAN WOMAN: And you didn't speak for several weeks.

DIEGO: That's right. We crossed the border. Chile disappeared; stayed behind. I didn't see it again for almost twenty years. I left my home. There was nobody back there; almost all our relatives and friends were too frightened, they never even wrote to me when I was in France. I thought that I had nobody in the entire world.

ASIAN WOMAN: *(Looking at him,*

intensively)

I want to scream...

DIEGO: *(Embraces her)*

ASIAN WOMAN: *(she holds on to him with all her strength, digs her nails into his arms, his shoulders - it looks as if she is gasping for air, living some internal agony)*

I want to scream, I want to scream...

DIEGO: Do it, if it will help.

(Expression of tremendous suffering on her face)

ASIAN WOMAN: I am afraid I can't.

DIEGO: *(gently)*

What did you just see, my love?

ASIAN WOMAN: *(Her face slowly relaxes)*

Her part in me... In my mind I just buried her family - her dead that are now also my dead... the people that stayed back on the island; those people you saw in front of the house; her family - my family... our family.

(Long howl of a ship's siren in the distance)

It's over now. It's over until we go back to my country. I am sure there will be more grief after we return. But I can't think about it now. I can't think about the burning streets and houses of my city. I can't accept that my city doesn't exist anymore.

DIEGO: I'm here. Squeeze me; bury your face in my chest. Cry if you can.

ASIAN WOMAN: No, it's better now. As long as you are here, I can go on living. Because you are not only my man, you are also my memory; you knew my country as it was before the war, you know what happened to it, to me; and to us.

(Her face gradually relaxes)

Will they ever learn how much pain they are sowing on this earth? Will they ever want to hear our stories? Or will their music get louder and louder and their movies sillier and sillier so they would never have to hear our screams?

DIEGO: I don't know. Sometimes I wonder myself...

ASIAN WOMAN: Now we have only each other.

DIEGO: But it's more than I ever hoped for. It's more than I ever had in my entire life.

ASIAN WOMAN: On one small tropical island, in a town reduced to ashes, two similar stories from two different parts of the world had united in one. Stories are always similar, no matter where on earth they occur. Us, the storytellers, have similar aims and similar means, too. The joy and pain have the same color and taste. And so has the compassion. Those who believe that they were appointed by god to spread divine justice by sword sent two of us – one man and one woman - on a seemingly endless journey of exile. They killed our families. Now we will have to learn how to walk again, how to live. It's two of us now, Diego; so at least there will be no solitude and no fear, anymore. And as we united, it seems that two of our countries are uniting as well. Your country accepted the pain of my land as its own pain. And later, I will take your parents; their dreams and their thoughts all the way across the ocean, to my city. You understood us and we will, no doubt, understand you. There is so much to learn from each other and so much to fight for. Both countries – yours and mine – are in essence those of dreamers and poets, of humble fishermen spreading their nets along the endless coastlines. Our people are shy and if alone, faced by the brutal force of greed and by unbridled desire to rule the world, they become defenseless. Unless united, we will always be defeated.

DIEGO: (*Very impressed, slowly*)

It will be an enormous adventure and a great honor to be by your side...

ASIAN WOMAN: And ours can still be a very good life, Diego.

DIEGO: (*Half mockingly*)

And you will never walk away, never disappear?

ASIAN WOMAN: (*Very seriously*)

Never, I swear.

(*He embraces her and she presses her face against his chest. This time her face is calm*)

(*Mother and Father enter through the open door. They are holding on to each other, like two lovers, talking to each other in a sarcastic, familiar and mocking way. They are each holding a glass of red wine in their hand. Nobody sees them; they are comfortably leaning against the wall of the bar. They look young, but from the way they are dressed and from the way they behave, it is obvious that they belong to a different decade. Their style is charming*).

FATHER: They look like us, forty years ago.

MOTHER: Full of hope and determination, and love. She is pretty and intelligent, if you will allow me to say so. But tell me, do you think that this time they will succeed? Do you think they will really be able to build a better world?

FATHER: (*Takes a sip from his glass, smiles at her*)

I don't know, Maria... maybe, maybe not. But look at them, they will do their best... and as long as they try, their lives will be full and worth living. Is there anything more exciting, more fulfilling than an attempt to improve the world?

(*Laughing*)

It's always better than to sit in the office, counting someone else's money!
And about succeeding in changing the world? It's not always about results; it's about the journey, the process itself. It's how it always was, for centuries: attempts and failures, but then again, new attempts...

MOTHER: I wish I could go with them...

FATHER: We will... We will finish our wine, Maria, and we will follow them.

(*Punches her, jokingly*)

Do you still remember the songs?

MOTHER: Yes, I remember the songs... and

the smell of tobacco on your shirt, and your hand holding mine, and the simple poems that you used to write on the napkins in the bars while waiting for me... and our first kiss... and our first victories.

FATHER: And the nights when it was raining and we were waiting for each other in front of the Turi Tower, before taking the Concepcion cable car... We used to walk a lot, back then. We used to talk and talk while walking, stopping in some small cafes and bars for a glass of wine or a hot cup of coffee.

MOTHER: (*Touching his face*)

Do you regret anything?

FATHER: No. I would do it all; all over again...with you.

(*Very seriously*)

And we won, Maria. They never did. They killed and destroyed, but they did it through violence and brutality. We won because the people trusted us, and because our songs and our poems were better.

MOTHER: And because we never did anything just for the sake of profit. We always loved this land with all its beauty and misery, we loved the men and women, honest and humble, living in the desert of the north, next to the slopes of steep mountains, by the ocean facing the waves, in the wooden houses buried under the snow. Whatever was done after us was done only because of greed, never because of love.

FATHER: But do *you* regret anything, Maria?

MOTHER: I regret that we died too young, but there is nothing one can do about it.

(He nods, smiling at her tenderly)

FATHER: You are still the most beautiful ghost on earth.

MOTHER: *(coquettishly running her fingers through her hair)*

Well, thank you. You don't look bad yourself, you know...

(The sounds of street fighting outside are growing louder. Sirens and some gun shots. Roar of the crowd. Whistles)

ASIAN WOMAN: I am scared, Diego...

DIEGO: So am I. I don't want to lose you now; the first day we met.

ASIAN WOMAN: But we have to go... They have the names of your parents on their lips. And there is almost nothing left of my city. We cannot waste time.

BOY STUDENT: Time to go!

GIRL STUDENT: (*Laughing happily*)

To the barricades, everybody!

1st SOLDIER: Let's go then... Damn it!

WAITER: (*Disappearing and reappearing shortly after with several uncorked bottles of wine*)

I am not going to the barricades sober! Wine and songs – the two best allies of any Latin revolution!

SPANISH WOMAN: (*Laughing*)

Don't forget the cheese, Enrique... some nice sharp one!

(*Waiter runs back to the kitchen, again*)

1st SOLDIER: (*Comes up to the Asian Woman*)

I was wrong, but I had no idea what I was doing. Please forgive me. Forgive me before we all go... there.

(*He nods towards the sounds of the fighting*)

(*She gives him a long look, then lifts her*

*hand and touches his chest with the palm of her hand. Then she nods and smiles at him, briefly. 1*ˢᵗ *Soldier is standing in front of her for a while, looking at the tips of his shoes)*

(Waiter re-emerges, holding something wrapped in the paper. Then he distributes wine among everybody)

WAITER: I have been waiting for this moment for thirty years! Thank you, God, and thank you for coming back, VICTORIA!

(Waiter lifts up his clenched fist to the air, with the paper-wrapped cheese in his hand)

*(Students and 1*ˢᵗ *Soldier are walking towards the door, followed by Victoria and the waiter, loud sound of the street fighting, sirens and bells of the church increases. Diego and the Asian Woman hold hands. They make their first steps, hesitantly. As they come closer to the door, they stop)*

ASIAN WOMAN: If we have to, we will fight for the memory of those we loved and lost; for their dreams... and for our own lives... For your land that is now mine and for my land that is yours.

DIEGO: And we will fight here, in Valparaiso, for your burning city!

There is suddenly a silence. The sounds of clashes disappear. The only sounds left are those of seagulls, wind and one long ship's siren, coming from the port.

Diego and the Asian Woman walk through the door, holding hands, without looking back. The Father and Mother are slowly following them and as they come closer to the door:

BLACKOUT

And

CURTAIN

Plays

Andre Vltchek

CONVERSATIONS WITH JAMES

Comedy in Six Acts

Andre Vltchek

PREFACE

I began writing *Conversations With James* in Jakarta, surrounded by enormous mosque, religious school and several smaller mosques called musholahs – all competing in producing mighty sounds, broadcasting calls for prayer, prayers themselves and whatever activity was taking place inside. Sounds were multiplied and carried all over the neighborhood through loudspeakers, scaring and depressing those few surviving atheists as well as people of different religions. Little girls, as young as 3, were being dragged by their overzealous parents to the biggest mosque for certain type of education. Not even George Orwell could envision more complete brainwashing scenario. It seemed that almost entire neighborhood thought the same way, behaved the same way, believed in the same religion. No alternatives seemed to be offered in the radius of several hundreds of miles.

Writing the play was an exercise on how to stay sane in the environment that I found antagonistic, even hostile to secularism, tolerance and reason. Unlike in Istanbul where artistic and beautiful calls for prayer (lasting only few minutes, five times a day) were evoking in me nostalgia and desire to learn more about the world so different from my own; gut-wrenching, badly crafted sounds coming from Jakarta mosques lasted well over five hours a day, stripped of beauty but leaving no doubt about who is really in complete control over the neighborhood.

Indonesia is a country where dissent was never tolerated; where hundreds of thousands of people belonging to Chinese minority were massacred after the 1965 military coup. Further hundreds of thousands were slaughtered for being "atheist" – almost all the leftists and progressives. The largest religious organization – NU – participated in the killings. Religious and ethnic cleansing continued in East Timor (where around one third of the population was exterminated) and in other parts of this unfortunate and violent archipelago.

I covered most violent of Indonesian pogroms as a journalist and I covered tens of other insane wars that had religious undertone: from the Middle East (Palestine/Israeli conflict) to Gujarat in India.

Almost all wars that I witnessed had something to do with religious believes: in God, in the final prophecy, in market fundamentalism, in emperor-God, in chosen nation, in supremacy of skin color, political or economic system.

It took me one year to write this play, much longer than previous political drama: *Ghosts of Valparaiso*. I labored over the dialogues on board of fast *shinkansen* trains in Japan, in remote South Pacific island nations possesses by Christian fundamentalist zeal, over foamy cappuccino in cafes of seemingly (but not necessarily) secular New Zealand and Australian cities.

And I finished writing it on Marshall Islands, in one of the most bizarre places on earth – on the biggest atoll our planet has – on Kwajalein. More precisely, on a small island called Ebeye, separated by just over one mile of water from enormous US star war military base; from inter-continental missile catchments.

While Kwajalein is hosting mighty radar installations, navigation equipment (and who knows what else; better not to ask...), as well as comfortable housing for the US military and civilian staff, Ebeye is synonymous to Micronesian hell – one of the most crammed places in the Pacific, with no running water and no waste management, with sporadic electricity supply; with children running barefoot - dirt and misery unseen almost anywhere else in this part of the world.

Despite appalling conditions on Ebeye, almost everyone there was a dedicated Christian often belonging to the most extreme and fanatical sects. No rebellion or revolution seemed to be in a pipeline. The same believes were shared across the water by those who were planning the Star Wars on Kwajalein. Despite all these hymns flying from the open doors of churches, celebrating sharing and love, entire place resembled tropical Micronesian South Africa during the apartheid.

I couldn't sleep in the only "decent" hotel on the island that became my home away from home for several days. There was no running water at night, no electricity. Combat platoons of roaches were invading my bed, crawling on top and under my sheets. One sleepless night I took my notebook and left hotel; parked myself in some coffee shop run by the migrant workers from Philippines, ordered something resembling coffee and finished writing this play.

For similar reason, I consider both Jakarta and Ebeye to be very appropriate places to begin and to finish this short, one act, comedy. And I am endlessly grateful to the people of Indonesia and The United States for pissing me off so deeply and violently, inspiring me and helping me to finish this little bitter comedy.

Andre Vltchek

CHARACTERS

GEORGE – playwright

JAMES – citizen of Elidia.

(*James is also known as God*)

GAIA – citizen of Elidia

VOICE OF RADIO ANNOUNCER

DRUNKS

INMATES OF INSANE ASYLUM

DOCTOR

THERE WILL BE NO INTERMISSION

ACT ONE

[Entire stage is in semi-darkness. A desk with computer monitor. Half-full bottle of red wine stands on top of the desk, close to the edge. GEORGE enters briskly, sits on the chair, stares at the monitor for a long while; and then gets up. He is pacing around the stage before returning to the table. He leans on its edges with both hands, before beginning to speak. His monologue is interrupted by short pauses]

GEORGE: I developed this habit... to talk to people on-line... typing the words or speaking to the microphone. When they use camera I can see their faces on my monitor. Images are often clear, but not always. Sometimes they are blurry. I got used to meeting total strangers in Internet chat rooms: some women, some men.

[He pours himself a glass of red wine; takes a sip]

GEORGE: Some women insist on showing me their breasts... or more. Others are just talking... about loneliness and ageing... touching impolite subjects they wouldn't dare to discuss even with their close friends. Others suggest real encounter... Intercourse... Caucasian women, Arab women, Asian women... Men have tendency to discuss women and politics. Almost all women prefer to discuss men...

[GEORGE takes deep sip of wine and holds the glass in his hand, observing the color. He slowly descends into the chair]

GEORGE: Then... one day... it happened. Without any warning... Unexpectedly.

[Short pause]

GEORGE: I had been sitting at my usual place, drinking wine like I am drinking it now, staring at the monitor. Some busty middle-aged nymphet was pouring her heart out to me... passed forty, can't find true love, scared she will have to stay alone for the rest of her life...

[Short pause]

GEORGE: ...Then everything went blank... And I heard terrible noise... Similar to fire-alarm, but not exactly like that of a fire-alarm...

[Loud noise. Similar to that of fire alarm, but not exactly like the fire alarm. GEORGE jumps from his chair, covers his ears, terrified expression on his face]

JAMES: [*his voice is metallic and it resonates somewhere above the stage*] Good evening, George!

GEORGE: Damn! What is it?! Who is it?! Who are you?! Where the hell are you?!

[*Another ringing sound, this time substantially shorter but more intensive than the previous one*]

JAMES: I am everything and I am everywhere, George. I am God!

GEORGE: [*Slightly taken aback but rapidly recovering his wits*]

Oh, stop it, would you?! God visiting me through the high-speed Internet connection?

JAMES: God, as I believe you were told, can visit you in any form.

GEORGE: You sound like some advanced computer virus.

JAMES: You don't seem to believe me.

GEORGE: Believe you what? That you are God?

JAMES: Yes... Yes, George... Believe me that I am your Creator. That's what God means to you, humans, doesn't he?

GEORGE: I don't believe in God.

JAMES: Right, George, of course you don't... That's absolutely fine. You don't have to believe in me. You don't even have to call me God.

GEORGE: How should I call you then?

JAMES: Call me anything... You can call me, for instance, James!

GEORGE: James?

JAMES: Yes, James. That's neutral, isn't it? Not too religious, not too secular. Neutral, I would say. Thoroughly acceptable for any imaginable purpose. You have to call me by some name, don't you? Then why not call me James?

GEORGE: James...

[*Has a swing straight from the bottle*]

What brings you here, James?

[*Short pause*]

JAMES: Desperation.

GEORGE: Desperation? Since when are gods desperate?

JAMES: [*Ignores his sarcasm*]

Frustration from being misunderstood.

GEORGE: [*looks dumb folded*]

Frustration...

JAMES: Desire to come clear... to tell the truth. Longing to confess...

GEORGE: [*sarcastically once again*]

Since when gods confess? I thought it is only we, common sinners, who are obliged to prostrate them and come clear in front of God!

JAMES: [*Modestly*]

Even God can have such desires.

GEORGE: [*Abruptly*]

James!..

JAMES: Yes?

GEORGE: Let's stop this silly game right now, please! You are not knocking at the right door. James, I don't believe in God! I am an atheist... And if you would be the Almighty, you would definitely know that.

JAMES: [*quietly*]

I do... I know. And I am an atheist myself.

GEORGE: [*First in shock, then laughing loudly*]

An atheist God! How thoroughly believable!

JAMES: [*Sadly*]

I am not blaming you for laughing... But I assure you...

GEORGE: I am running out of time, James. I am in the middle of writing my latest atheist play. And I was just trying to arrange a date with a desperate lady who is in great and urgent need for certain emotional and physical consolation.

JAMES: I know all that. I apologize for taking your time. But allow me to reveal that I contacted you exactly because I am truly enjoying the play that you are presently writing. Forgive me for reading from behind your back... and from your mind... George, seriously, if you need any proof...

GEORGE: Proof of what?

JAMES: You know... The proof... That I am what I say I am.

GEORGE: [*Suddenly very interested*]

What kind of proof can you offer?

JAMES: Any proof you will ask for.

GEORGE: Show your face!

JAMES: I have many faces. I can choose any face. I can choose any body, any form. I can be a woman or a man. I can be a child. I can take a form of gentle breeze or I can batter a shore like the most vicious storm.

GEORGE: Show your real face.

JAMES: I don't have one. Or... I do, but nothing that you humans could comprehend. I live in quite different dimensions. If I show you my real face; you will probably see absolutely nothing. Or you will see something that may appear very disturbing, even terrible.

GEORGE: Then wouldn't it be fair to say that for us, humans, you simply do not exist?

JAMES: That would be a simplification, to a certain extend...

GEORGE: [*Suddenly smiles*]

If I can't see real you, then send someone... a person I would really like to meet. Try to read my dreams. Can't you read my mind? You should, if you are genuine God.

JAMES: [*Thinks for a while, then begins to mumble*]

I am your creator... Let me try then... Person you really want to meet... Petite, Asian, not too young and not too old... Impeccably dressed... Long hair...

[*George seems to be lost in thoughts. Lights become progressively dimmer. James continues mumbling incomprehensively. It goes on for almost one entire minute. Then suddenly loud knock on the door. GEORGE is shaken by the sound. He jumps from his chair, runs to open the door. Before he can, there is another knock*]

GEORGE: Who is it?

[*No answer. George opens the door sharply and decisively. GAIA walks in. She is Asian, petite, elegant, not too young and not too old, dressed impeccably. Her long black hair is falling in graceful disorder to her shoulders*]

GEORGE: [*Apparently shaken*]

Oh my God!

JAMES: [*From above, suddenly sarcastically*]

Exactly!

GAIA: [*Her voice is very gentle and very feminine*]

In case you are wondering, I am also a god. But call me Gaia. James created me on a spare of the moment, out of your dreams. I am the woman you always wanted to meet but never did.

GEORGE: [*Unable to speak. He walks to her, extends his hands but stops short from touching her. Suddenly he falls on his knees, squeezes her hips in his palms and presses his face against her thighs. She begins caressing his hair*]

Oh my God!

JAMES: George, for heaven's sake; brace yourself! I came to talk to you... I traveled through the galaxies, enduring speed higher than light... I feel jetlagged and my body aches. I need massage. Let go of her and let's discuss important matters.

GEORGE: [*Begging*]

Don't take her away from me!

JAMES: [*Impatient*]

Fine, George, you can have her. She can stay with you. Now would you sit down and listen, please?

[*GEORGE walks slowly back to his chair. GAIA follows him. When he sits down, she stays behind his chair, still caressing his hair*]

Can I speak now?

GEORGE: Please... Please do!

[PAUSE, then BLACKOUT]

JAMES: We fucked up, George!

Andre Vltchek

ACT TWO

[*Loud and terrible ringing sound, similar to that of fire alarm, but not exactly of fire alarm. Stage is dark for as long as the ringing sound lasts. Then the lights come slowly back. GAIA is sitting on the chair, one leg elegantly bend; her skirt is up above her knees. Her underwear is resting on the arm of one of the chairs*]

GEORGE: I experienced heaven!

[*Long ringing sound again*]

JAMES: [*His voice is coming, as in the previous act, from somewhere above the ceiling*]

You humans are so physical and so predictable! We created you like that, of course. We needed you to multiply... But your lust exceeded all our expectations. It is so ridiculous, so comical to watch you from above!

GEORGE: Thank you, James... Now I believe!

JAMES: [*Impatiently*]

Rubbish! Believe in what? Let's cut all that human sentimental nonsense and get to the core. You needed to copulate and we created a suitable mate for your copulation. We did some quick calculations, planning, designing. We converted one of our sisters... She is now a perfect size and shape for you; exactly compatible with your body and with your preferences. There is no mystery in all that. Are you listening, George?

GEORGE: I am listening to you, oh James! Your wisdom knows no boundaries.

JAMES: Good.

[*Pause*]

George?

GEORGE: I am listening.

JAMES: There is no God.

GEORGE: Oh...

JAMES: Do you understand what I am saying? Can I find at least someone among you, humans, who would be able to comprehend this simple message?

GEORGE: I am trying, but...

JAMES: But? I will allow her to explain. When I speak, it takes too much energy... Thousands of light-years, you know...

[*Ringing sound, this time very short one, then silence. GAIA pulls down her skirt. She takes her panties to the right hand and gets up briskly. Throughout the monologue, she is playing with the panties*]

GAIA: When he speaks, it takes too much energy. It is easier if I explain.

[*GEORGE is sitting on the floor, looking at GAIA, dumb and adoring expression on his face, staring directly at her lips as she speaks. Her monologue is delivered in a matter of fact voice*]

We came here from far-away galaxy, from a small planet in the solar system unknown to you, humans. Our society is extremely developed but even we had to go through the complex evolution. At some point we managed to create just and egalitarian society. Our beings know no pain. Our lives became eternal. We can change our appearance in order to please each other. We don't age, we can shrink and expand, we can swim and we can fly. Knowledge of each of us is almost limitless. But we were dreaming about other forms of life and other galaxies. We designed and built spaceships and embarked on epic journeys. Later we learned how to move in space on our own. But we still couldn't find our brothers and sisters in this vast universe. Then one of our supreme sisters came up with the idea to create new form of life in your solar system. We triggered what you call "Big Bang"; then we implanted the most primitive organisms to the water of your oceans. These were organisms that were predestined to evolve into what you became now: human beings.

GEORGE: [*Still from the floor*]

Amazing! I always considered this to be a possibility!

GAIA: Entire process had been designed by what you, humans, would call our great scientists. But our most refined thinkers, our philosophers, artists and dreamers also helped to program you. They were burning with desire to create something pure, even irrational: beings with tremendous capacity for tenderness, kindness and compassion.

GEORGE: I understand...

JAMES: [*The silence is suddenly interrupted by loud and metallic voice*]

But we fucked up!!!

GAIA: [*Pragmatically, in a matter-of-fact voice*]

Yes, we fucked up endlessly. As you were evolving as species, elements of greed and violence were becoming predominant in your character. One thing was becoming absolutely clear: our scientists and poets simply miscalculated.

GEORGE: I suspected that.

GAIA: We were watching from great distance in horror... We were watching how you began slaughtering each other over meaningless things. Men raping women and cutting throats of their own brothers: over the land, over money, over power. Entire clans vanishing... Human flesh consumed by fellow humans. Greed had suddenly no boundaries.

[*GAIA comes briskly close to George, puts her palm under his shirt and begins caressing his chest. Then she, abruptly, pushes him away*]

We had to intervene somehow. But we were too far away. We could have stopped the experiment – put final end to it - but that would mean annihilation of the human race. We had turbulent discussions on that matter but when it came to voting, great majority decided that your species gained undeniable right to exist and it would be thoroughly immoral on our part to liquidate you.

GEORGE: [*From the floor*]

But why did you not try to communicate with us?

GAIA: We did. That's exactly what we were trying to do for centuries. With negligible result...

[*She comes close to him. He prostrates himself on the floor, spreading his arms and legs, face up. She slowly puts the heel on his chest, then teasingly pokes his chin with the tip of the pointed shoe*]

We did, George. We contacted your people on many occasions, but were always misunderstood. It started with the Torah, but maybe even earlier. Then we pampered one of the human's brightest children. We explained to him the essence of egalitarian society, equal distribution of wealth and advantages that come with it... He went around explaining, carrying our message, but you put him on the cross so at the end we had to spend what you would call trillions of megawatts of energy, moving him to our galaxy and giving him political asylum.

[*GAIA sights desperately*]

Instead of learning anything about the social structures, you created religion around him – something he was explicitly telling you not to do! Hundreds of years later, when your wars were becoming increasingly monstrous, we contacted another bright son of your species, explaining to him that we are considering to stop the experiment in order to safe the humanity from excessive suffering... Through him, we gave your species one last warning. But that message was misunderstood as well, and the last warning had been changed to the last prophecy! And our message got misinterpreted on many counts.

[*GAIA begins pacing up and down the room in anger*]

At the end, when the situation became thoroughly unbearable, we decided to approach the greatest thinker of that time. That was in the middle of total insanity, when European powers were dividing entire world, colonizing every single piece of land on your planet, treating people of other races like slaves. We tried to explain to him that things are moving beyond good and evil as the humans see them, and that there is no God and there had never been one. He considered our message for several years; then came up with conclusion that "God is dead!"

GEORGE: [*Howls*]

We had such high hopes for him!

GAIA: By then there was not one inch of the world that was free, almost everything under the boot of colonizing soldiers. And then...

[*GAIA gasps*]

... And then they began killing each other on their own continent. Concentration camps and battlefields resembling enormous slaughterhouses...

GEORGE: ...And now...

GAIA: And now, despite all that so-called progress, majority of people on your planet lives in total filth and gutter. Thieves and deceivers are ruling your world, by naked greed. Local elites took over from former colonial masters, becoming even more brutal and merciless. Most of the people on your planet are still living in feudal societies, some are even experiencing slavery... And in the rich world? You threw your best minds to insane asylums, marginalized them; made them irrelevant. There is no compassion left on your planet.

[*She stops; pauses for a few moments, apparently lost in thoughts*]

We were aiming at the masterpiece. But we made some terrible mistakes. We have to stop this... Somehow. Soon.

JAMES: [*His metallic voice above the ceiling once again*]

Now!!!

GAIA: [*In a natural voice*]

Now. Probably now.

[*Short pause*]

Because your own people are suffering. Because, despite all that propaganda, more and more beings on your planet are exploited, robbed of everything, divided, neutralized. Your rulers are exercising such complete control over the world that no revolt, no rebellion is possible anymore. It is the endgame for your civilization.

GEORGE: But what will you do now? Nuke us?

[*GAIA lowers herself to the floor. She lies on top of him, pressing her entire body against his*]

GAIA: We can love you to death... Or we can...

JAMES: Nonsense! We need consensus of your species. We need someone to explain to them that what is happening to them now is... a result of an experiment that went terribly wrong!

GAIA: [*Kisses George on his lips*]

And that is why we came to you...

JAMES: Because you will be the one to tell them.

GAIA: To explain to them...

JAMES: To ask them what do they want us to do?

GAIA: We can recall... We can stop the entire thing if your people decide that's what they want us to do. You can all vanish quickly and painlessly...

JAMES: Or we can share our technology. We can explain to you how to grow more food, how to effectively purify and desalinate ocean water, how to move from one place to another fast, efficiently and without polluting the environment.

GAIA: We can offer medicine that could cure all your diseases and make you live for at least 500 years. We can help you to design egalitarian society.

JAMES: We can do all that and much more, but we are not sure that our ideas would be welcomed. It seems that your species are not interested in justice and harmony... Your world is obsessed with money, hungry for power... Those who are choking your world will not be willing to give up their privileges for the good of majority. Apparently competing with others and exercising power brings the strongest of you more joy than living in harmonious society.

GEORGE: No doubt about it.

GAIA: We are afraid that it may be the case...

JAMES: But we have to try, George!

[*Dramatic pause*]

Would you like to be our new prophet?

GEORGE: Me?.. But...

[*Confused, almost terrified look appears on his face*]

GAIA: [*Comes close to him, looking straight to his eyes. Each step she makes is a masterpiece of eroticism and elegance combined*]

George?

GEORGE: [*Begins to tremble looking at her*]

Gaia... I don't know if I can...

GAIA: [*Stands over George, his face right between her feet*]

Look. Look up!

[*George looks up. He loses control, his palms grab her calves*]

GAIA: We need you, George! Humanity needs you.

GEORGE: [*His internal struggle doesn't last long. Staring right above him, he finally shouts:*]

Oh yes! I will. I will!

BLACKOUT

Andre Vltchek

ACT THREE

[*The same as in the previous acts. Lights are slowly beginning to illuminate the stage. One light points to the computer table. GEORGE is sitting at the table, facing the monitor. GAIA is resting in the chair, which is lost in a shadow*]

GEORGE: [*Mumbling*]

Fourteen million, seven hundred thousand and twenty-five dollars!

[*He is moving computer mouse, staring at the monitor in disbelieve*]

I had only sixty-eight dollar and five cents in my checking account yesterday!

GAIA: We suspected that in order to carry on your mission successfully you might need some substantial funds. We can, of course, supply you with much more...

GEORGE: [*Confused*]

But... So much money...

GAIA: Prophet is very important being. He tells millions of people what to do and to restrain from. You may need to hire a jet... or to pay hundreds of scribbles to put your discourses on the paper... to buy decent car. Your species don't trust poor honest blokes, George. They like shiny vehicles, snow-white false dentures and neatly tailored jackets. You look like slop, if you don't mind me saying so. We need to go out and buy you new pair of designer glasses, expensive looking watch and several pair of shoes.

GEORGE: [*Obviously hurt*]

What's wrong with my glasses and my watch?

GAIA: They look... ordinary.

GEORGE: I selected them myself. They are part of me. I like them.

GAIA: You need to look imposing... Impressive... Important. They have to trust you and they have to envy you. They even have to fear you. You see; I did my homework before coming here.

GEORGE: [*Ironically*]

Should I pull all my teeth out and instead get perfect looking implants?

GAIA: [*Not catching his irony*]

That's awfully thoughtful of you, George! You are a fast learner. We should arrange for it. You see, you have to appeal to the masses. You will have to convince them that there is no God, only us. They may not like your words, because they believed for centuries in Almighty fatherly figures. You will have to tell them the truth. And remember: nothing scares and disgusts human beings more than the truth!

GEORGE: But I myself don't know the truth.

GAIA: That's why I am here. To explain... To guide you... To answer all your questions...

[*She stands up and slowly walks to him. She spreads her arms, stopping just a few steps before GEORGE*]

Ask! Ask me anything!

GEORGE: [*Deep in thoughts*]

Anything?

GAIA: Anything!

GEORGE: Have you also approached Karl Marx?

GAIA: Of course! He was one of our best disciples. He understood...

[*Pause*]

...Although not everything.

GEORGE: Lenin?

GAIA: Yes, but he understood much lesser than Marx. Although he had some good organizing skills.

GEORGE: Che?

GAIA: By then we were already quite desperate, of course... But he turned out to be one of the best. But he had asthma. We offered to fly him home to Elidia... We offered to cure him so he might be more effective, but he refused. He was a purist, believing exclusively in Latin-style revolution... and in liberation of Africa. He wasn't thrilled to learn about the project, about the fact that we created the world. It was clashing with his theories. But at the end we managed to forge very fruitful cooperation. Anyway, we had to resurrect him as well. He is now in Elidia with the rest....

GEORGE: Stalin?

GAIA: Definitely not! Have some fate in our moral judgment.

GEORGE: [*suddenly screams in frustration*]

But why me?!

GAIA: [*Taken aback*]

But you are brilliant...

GEORGE: Many people are. I am womanizer... Between us...

[*He whispers*]

...Between us, I care about sex more than I care about social justice. I write plays in order to impress women. I am not as good as you think I am.

GAIA: [*Consoling him*] Nobody is good. Nobody was ever good. Besides, you don't need any other woman right now. We took care of that part. I should be fully sufficient. Now you can concentrate on your mission.

GEORGE: I belong to the Left out of spite for the Right!

GAIA: Does it really matter? As long as you are on correct side of the barricade, as you humans say...

GEORGE: Tell me more... why me?

GAIA: You don't believe in anything, don't have any dogma.

GEORGE: Most of educated people in this world believe in nothing.

GAIA: We... We simply liked you! We read your books; we followed you around for some time.

GEORGE: [*Hitting his forehead*]

You did? How embarrassing!

GAIA: Don't worry! We are different species. And after all, we are responsible for all your weaknesses. We created you, although indirectly. We are like... almost like your parents.

GEORGE: [*Sarcastically*]

I do certain things I wouldn't want my mother to witness!

GEORGE: [*Ignoring his irony*]

We created the molecules...

GEORGE: So the old Darwin was correct...

GAIA: Definitely... To a large extend.

GEORGE: Not fully?

GAIA: We tried to perform some tune-up when we realized that the things are not going all too well. Darwin couldn't know that. He believed that the evolution was uninterrupted, natural process.

GEORGE: Then I have one more question: who created you?

GAIA: We are children of the similar experiment. We were created by more advanced species. We are result of more successful experiment I have to admit.

GEORGE: Then who created "them"?

GAIA: Others. It was a continuous process. Call it universal evolution. Advanced species achieved perfection and immortality. They built egalitarian societies with no burning problems, no worries, no diseases and no pain. But life has sense only because of its imperfections; when all goals are achieved, meaning of our existence disappears. Struggle for better world gives purpose to our life, to your life, to any life... Lack of challenges creates eternal boredom, even some sort of desperation. This is exactly what happened to us but also to those who created our species many millions of years earlier... and to those who created them billions of years ago. It is never about the goals and results, George... It is always about the journey, about the process. We fight revolutions, we build and we create new concepts. When there is nothing to improve anymore, life looses its meaning...

GEORGE: So after creating perfect societies, they and you decided to vanish. But before...

GAIA: I knew that for human being you are very bright. Yes, that's exactly what has happened. We felt obliged to create new life that would continue inhabiting this universe after our departure. Except that... in this particular case...or more precisely, in your case...

JAMES: [*From above the stage, producing desperate and loud scream*]

We fucked up!!!

BLACKOUT

ACT FOUR

[There is almost no PAUSE between the ACTS 3 and 4. During the BLACKOUT, which lasts approximately one minute, there are sounds of loud explosions and shouts of military commands, then the VOICE OF NEWS ANNOUNCER. Light gradually returns. GEORGE and GAIA are still in the same position as in the ACT THREE]

VOICE OF NEWS ANNOUNCER: ...US and coalition troops were bombarding positions of the terrorist groups that were earlier demanding nationalization of all natural resources in their country; demand which the White House described as dangerous, undermining democracy and basic principles of the free world. Groups were also pressing for release of their leader, Francisco Gonzalez, who is presently held in custody at the US military-base in Haiti, used to interrogate terrorist suspects. Two years ago, Mr. Gonzalez gain his notoriety by organizing protest matches all over Latin America, calling for withdrawal of the troops from the Coalition of Giving that invaded Venezuela several months earlier. New Delhi: Protesters clashed with the riot police, after international arbitrary court ruled that multi-national pharmaceutical conglomerate – Fotzer – acted legally when copyrighting Yoga earlier this year. Sudan: Almost 3 million refugees...

[*GEORGE hits the button on his computer and the broadcast gets interrupted*]

GEORGE: I think that plenty of people on this planet would rather live decent and eternal life in egalitarian society than... than this... What should I call it...

JAMES: [*From above*]

Shiiiiiit!!!!!!!!

GAMES: Exactly. Thank you, James. You are always an inspiration...

GAIA: That's why we are here.

GEORGE: It took you... some time.

GAIA: It is not so simple, George. Even in our advanced society we have plenty of members who believe in what you call "political correctness". In Elidia it is brought to a different level, but the essence is similar. For instance some thinkers thought for centuries that we have no right to lecture others, even if our civilization is much more advanced. They believed that you should have full control over your destiny. They were willing to allow you to butcher millions of your people, hoping that eventually you will get wise and invent your own wheel. They insisted on respecting your culture.

GEORGE: How considerate of them.

GAIA: But things are rapidly changing. Now there is almost absolute consensus that the experiment went too far. That your species will never be able to create just and equal society without the intervention from outside, and that unless you will be stopped, you will continue massacring millions of defenseless beings annually, while keeping great majority of your population in a gutter. Not to speak about other species that inhabit your planet. Not to speak about the environment. So now we are here. And the first thing we want to do is to tell your people the truth. They have to learn how to think rationally. They have to learn how to live without the anesthetics - without religions - facing uncomfortable truth that there is no god and no higher meaning of life... only us.

GEORGE: [*Ironically*]

But why would you go so far out of your way?

GAIA: We felt compassion...

JAMES: [*From above the stage*]

She already explained it to you: we want to depart! Let's be honest: we want to get out, and we want to be sure that you could take over. We either have to improve your species, or we have to delete you and start from the scratch. Second option would mean that we have to stick around for further tens of millions of years.

GAIA: What James is saying is that we would like to rest; too tired of living eternally. But we can't depart, yet. If we do, you humans will be the only thinking beings left in the universe!

JAMES: And that would be very unsettling prospect.

GEORGE: Unfortunately I have to agree.

GAIA: Because you people are...

JAMES: Piiiiiiigs!!!! Thieves!!!!! Rapists!!!!! Mass murderers. Greedy bandits! Primitives...

GAIA: What James means is that you people are not yet suitable to be sole masters of the universe.

JAMES: They shouldn't be allowed to master even their own farts!

GAIA: James, you are being too

graphic...

JAMES: [*To GEORGE*]

Tell them.

GEORGE: [*Suddenly angry*]

Tell them what?

JAMES: Tell them how it all happened...

GEORGE: [*Increasingly irritated*]

How can I tell them? I don't know anything. I never even saw you. Again, I have to believe in what you tell me, but where is the proof? I am expected to believe that you actually exist, but as you know, I am not good at... at believing. You sent me a perfect lover, but is that enough of a proof? Tell me more. Convince me. Show your face, James!

JAMES: My face??

[*Laughs*]

You really want to see it?

GEORGE: I have to... I can't help you otherwise.

[*Short PAUSE*]

GAIA: ...no.

JAMES: [*Ignores her distress*]

Very well then. Come to the kitchen, George. It will cost tremendous amount of energy, but I am willing to use it, just in order to convince you. And remember, whatever you see there... it is me, but scaled down ten million times. Brought to your dimensions, so to speak. And each of us is slightly different. But at least you will get some general idea. Are you ready, George?

[*GEORGE slowly stands up*]

GEORGE: Ready.

[*He is slowly but steadily walking towards the door. He opens it, switches on the light, then short PAUSE*]

GAIA: [*Suddenly terrified*]

No!!! Come back, George!

[*GEORGE ignores her outburst; closes the door behind him. GAIA stares at the door in terror. Long PAUSE. Then desperate, loud shout. GEORGE is screaming in unrecognizable voice. Something falls.*]

GEORGE: Oh no! No!!!!!

[*He howls. Door flies open. GEORGE, his hair standing on his head is rolling on the floor. He enters living room in rolling motion, still screaming. Eventually he stops and sits down on the floor. He is breathing heavily. He seems to be uncertain whether he will begin to puke or whether he will die from suffocation. Eventually he slowly comes back to his senses. His breathing normalizes, but he is still sitting cross-legged on the floor, look of disbelief on his face*]

GEORGE: [*To the ceiling*]

Now I understand, James! Your species should definitely depart this universe. What kind of bastard created you?

[*PAUSE*]

Now I understand, therefore I believe, James!

[*Finally he is overwhelmed by the nausea. He crawls to the corner, gets on all four and pukes loudly*]

BLACKOUT

ACT FIVE

[*A pub. Semi-darkness. Several drunks are sitting at three simple wooden tables, facing television set. Monitor of the set is turned away from the stage. Pre-recorded voice of GEORGE*]

GEORGE: ...And then they wrote down some simple rules that are easy to comprehend. You shall not kill thy neighbor. Don't rape your friend's wife...

1st DRUNK: [*Laughing*] ...your friend's wife! What if you don't fancy having friends?

GEORGE: Don't...

ALL DRUNKS: [*In unison, overshooting television set*]

...Don't steal from the poor... don't lie to the masses! Don't sow false hopes...

1st DRUNK: But that is what they are doing to us. All we are allowed to do now is to bitch about the way this world is arranged, as long as our bitching is not too loud and doesn't lead to action. They call it freedom of speech and democracy. We can go and vote for one of their candidates. All candidates that make it to the top must be benign; pre-approved by establishment that controls media, all major political parties, everything. We can even stay at home and not vote at all; it would not matter.

GEORGE: ...When Elidians realized it wouldn't work, they created a prototype man. Call him special edition human. They tried to prevent greed taking over the planet. To prevent what happened later anyway: business interests creating invisible coups against democracy, the upgraded street-vendors ruining decency, compassion and kindness. But the humans nailed him – that special edition - to the cross and kept stealing, raping and murdering as if there was no tomorrow. Few centuries later Elidians pampered another human prototype, but this time they did some serious PR. They flew him first few solar years to Elidia, showing him very posh accommodations up there, as well as certain amount of women shaped to his liking. They told him that he should be forceful in his preaching: to promise and to warn! You see; it didn't work either, as the new religion began expanding through its own colonial wars all over Arabia, North Africa and Indian sub-continent. In the meantime, the followers of the bloke who ended up on the cross continued launching their own colonial adventures, worldwide... Both sides are at odds until now.

2nd DRUNK: [*Extending his hand holding the pint of beer*]

To their health then! Cheers!

GEORGE: You see; Elidians tried their

best. When they realized that religions brought only wars and intellectual decay, they decided to talk to that big, fat, bearded German and also to his buddy who happened to be another bearded German whose father owned the factory... But even that didn't help. Attempts to create rational, equal and compassionate society on the Planet Earth were simply failing. Eventually things went out of control. Humanity never managed to shed-off its primitive believes. They kept killing each other again and again in the name of God. Christians killing pagans, Muslims killing North Africans, then Christians killing Muslims and Muslims killing Christians. Later Hindus killing Muslims and Muslims killing Hindus, while Christians killed everybody they could find on their path. Then Muslims killing Muslims: Shiites killing Sunnis and vice versa. Catholics killing Protestants and vice versa. Catholics and Protestants in unison killing Jews. Jews killing Muslims and Muslims killing Jews and other infidels.

1st DRUNK: Religions may be not much more than rubbish, but there is definitely some god! If not, our life would become meaningless. We don't want to believe in other beings that are in essence like ourselves, even if they are more advanced. We need an Almighty father, frightening and tremendous, thundering, punishing but also on occasions forgiving. We need to prostrate ourselves at his feet. We need to prostrate ourselves, period! We need to kiss his toes, to lick his anus, to gratefully inhale his farts. We need to feel that we are nothing while he is everything... therefore... indirectly... passing entire responsibility for our actions to Him... thinking that we are nothing more than ants in his forest; some stinky crap, weak, miniscule and negligible creatures.

2nd DRUNK: Yes! And knowing what shits we are, we need to believe that there is something splendid and noble hanging above us. Nothing concrete, nothing real... Just abstract, scary and unreachable... And we need religion to lie to us, to promise to us that this something actually exists. And when we believe, it is much easier to steal, to cheat, to rape, even to murder! When we believe we can always expect that we will be eventually purified and forgiven. We can think that to God our crimes matter lesser than our efforts to prostrate, chant, kneel and humiliate ourselves...

1st DRUNK: ...But if we don't believe, than facing oneself in the morning... looking at the mirror: a thief is just a thief... a rapist is a rapist... crook is a crook! That's why the most compassionate and sharing and orderly nations are atheist... and the most bigoted, brutal, compassionless are those possessed by religious zeal!

2nd DRUNK: But we can't allow these ideas to get hold of our society!

[*All drunks began to argue, screaming at each other. Suddenly one of them smashes his pint against the floor. Deep silence*]

A DRUNK: Are authorities blind? That terrorist George is confusing us! He has to be stopped and brought to Haiti for further investigation! The essence of our freedom and democracy and way of life is closely linked to religion.

1st DRUNK: Even if he is right, George is insane!

[*Loud metallic voice, not unlike fire alarm. Drunks stop arguing, panic is reflected on their faces. To absolute silence, JAMES begins to laugh, loudly and scornfully*]

BLACKOUT

ACT SIX

[Mental institution. Slow, retarded, senile musac. Two inmates in the uniform of the institution are aimlessly pacing back and forth. GEORGE is also wearing institution's uniform. He is sitting on the plastic chair, staring to the distance. Young female DOCTOR appears on the stage. Her voice is cheerful and optimistic, but her face is covered by veil and only her eyes are visible]

DOCTOR: Good morning, everybody!

GEORGE: Good morning, Doc!

[Two other inmates are ignoring both of them. Musac is slowly decreasing in volume and eventually disappears altogether]

DOCTOR: How do you feel today, George?

GEORGE: Just fine, thank you. I had been thinking about what you said the other day... About the relativity of knowledge... How different people can interpret information in various ways.

DOCTOR: Good, George... And?

GEORGE: And...

DOCTOR: You had no further contact with Gaia or James?

GEORGE: They never came back.

DOCTOR: [*Sighs*]

That's pity. I have some very bad news, George. Your bank launched an investigation soon after coming to conclusion that by error 14 million dollars had been transferred to your account. You apparently went on unbridled spending spree.

GOERGE: I...

DOCTOR: You hired Learjet and flew to Africa, to preach social equality and atheism to Nigerians. After that you attempted to land in Riyadh but Saudi authorities didn't allow you to even touch their holy runway with your infidel landing gear. You then flew to Tel Aviv, throwing enormous party at...

GEORGE: True! I was instructed to...

DOCTOR: Here we go again!

GEORGE: I spoke to the masses in Africa, Latin America and Europe. I secured huge following in Japan and India. What I was saying was rational; it made sense. Religions were and are ruining the world and they always stand on the side of the oppressors. Elidians, not some Almighty in heavens, created human beings. There is no heaven and no hell, only ceaseless boredom if we manage to live eternally...

DOCTOR: You used money that didn't belong to you.

GEORGE: Elidians transferred the money.

DOCTOR: Unfortunately that's not what the president of your bank says. According to her, you managed to spend 5 million dollars, two hundred and two thousand five hundred and twelve dollars... and forty-seven cents, to be precise. That's what they claim you owe them right now, George.

GEORGE: But I was told...

DOCTOR: Again, George? The Elidians told you? Do you have anything in writing; anything that can prove that they transferred funds? Do you still believe in them?

GEORGE: I don't believe in anything, Doc. I saw them with my own eyes. I saw the monstrous leader of their mission: James. I conversed with him. I saw Gaia, one of their women... or more precisely, a woman they created from my own dreams. My woman... The most beautiful and desirable being I ever encountered in my life and whom I miss tremendously... I spoke to both of them: we really had long and fruitful conversations. I made love to Gaia, several times a day. I don't believe in them, I experienced them.

DOCTOR: [*Reading from her notepad*]

You went to London and managed to get yourself invited to one of the BBC talk shows. It earned you immediately fatwa from the Muslims, excommunication from the Catholic Church...

GEORGE: How could they excommunicate me from something I never belonged to?

DOCTOR: Furthermore it earned you condemnation from Hindus, Judaists, Buddhists and other forty-eight religions and sects. You didn't get much sympathy even from the Scientologists!

GEORGE: Not surprisingly...

DOCTOR: Not surprisingly, maybe... But the bottom-line is that you gained no friends at all. Even Marxists were not too thrilled: they attacked you for your profound nihilism and for spite for the human race... The only kind words came from anarchists and supporters of euthanasia.

GEORGE: I know, I know... At least someone can think rationally.

[*Mockingly*]

But was it ever easy to be a prophet?

DOCTOR: Well, well... Some prophets had it easier, as I recall.

[*Once again turning pages of her notebook*]

Not able to convince the masses by common means of communication, you succumbed to extreme actions. You invited one hundred top European writers and intellectuals. You rented a ballroom in Paris, climbed to banquet table and attempted to urinate to an ancient Chinese vase – an act described as culturally insensitive. You got drunk and began insulting free market economics, mass media, pop culture as well as all major and minor religions of the world. You drew a parallel between the President of the United States and anal opening. You offered one million dollars and a Ferrari for the best atheist poem.

GEORGE: I was getting desperate. I agree I probably went overboard!

DOCTOR: [*Her eyes in the notebook*]

Possibly...

[*Suddenly she leans towards him and whispers*]

They used you, George!

GEORGE: I did what they asked me to do. I did it because they made sense. Why did they allow this to happen? Why am I in this shit-hole of a mental institution? Why am I broke? I never asked for their money and I never used it for my personal gain.

DOCTOR: [*Whispers*]

I gather they never needed you to win, just to begin the struggle. And they sacrificed you in the process. They used you to sow the seeds of doubt... There will be others coming after you. Many years from now you will be remembered as the first human who grasped the truth. You will be celebrated, revered and admired. Many years from now, as I said... Decades after you will be dead.

GEORGE: [*Sarcastically*]

What a great honor it will be! Why didn't they airlift me to Elidia like Karl Marx and Che?

DOCTOR: Apropos, how did she look like?

GEORGE: Who?

DOCTOR: Don't be a fool... Gaia.

GEORGE: She...

[*He begins drawing the curves in the air, using both hands*]

She...

DOCTOR: [*Takes off her veil*]

Like this?

GEORGE: Be I damned! You didn't leave me?

[*Grabs her hand*]

GAIA/DOCTOR: They exiled me!

GEORGE: Why?

GAIA: No particular reason. But I suspect that from their point of view I got too contaminated by your human habits, after spending several days in the human form and shape and in your company.

[*She pauses*]

You people always believed that the God, gods or any higher beings have to be good and moral and kind. Reality is that...

JAMES: ... That we are absolute shiiiiiits, too!!!!

GAIA: [*Sadly*]

James is departing...

GEORGE: James!

[*Two inmates stop pacing on the stage. They look at GEORGE in bewilderment. Both begin to knock their fingers at their temples, smiling with benevolent and understanding expression on their faces]*

GAIA: But one thing is unfortunately obvious: there is no God, only us, beings like James. I am beginning to wonder whether it is even necessary to spread this news among the humans. It may be better to live in deceit...

GEORGE: What will happen to us now?

GAIA: What will happen to the humanity? Who cares, really?

GEORGE: No, not to the humanity! To us: to you and me?

GAIA: Well, we will escape, will we not? And we will do that one thing that I truly enjoyed doing... Enjoyed much more than living sterile eternal life in Elidia. That thing you and I were doing day and night... That in and out that you humans call sex. Eventually we will get old, catch some disease and die. Isn't it fantastic?!

GEORGE: We are broke. Bank is chasing me!

GAIA: We will manage. I have stolen some codes... and some know-how. I will be able to traffic some funds to your account once we get our hands on some wired computer.

GEORGE: My account is blocked.

GAIA: We will open a new one. We will change your name and move to Rio or Nairobi.

GEORGE: [*Suddenly desperate*]

Gaia, I got accustomed carrying on higher mission! I actually enjoyed being a prophet. Are you telling me that from now on we will be just copulating, eating, defecating and sleeping? Like the rest of them? Am I not going to fight against religions, anymore? Am I not going to tell the truth, anymore? The truth that there is no God and that all religions are build on lies and keep human beings in ignorance and poverty, igniting intolerance and violence?

GAIA: That would be dangerous and it wouldn't be necessary. You already completed your mission. Now we can rest. Rest and enjoy life. You can live comfortably for the rest of your days. Wouldn't you enjoy some golfing and yachting for a change? Some caviar and buckets of first-rate champagne? First-rate masseuses and the fastest cars your species ever built? Or maybe little corporate jet? Or a villa overlooking dramatic cliff and endless ocean?

GEORGE: [*In despair*]

I need to talk to James! In order to live I need much more than just fulfilling of my bodily functions. I need to struggle! I need my life to have some deeper meaning. One needs to submit to God or one needs to fight against God! Try to find God or attempt to prove that there is no God!

JAMES: [*His voice suddenly coming from the great distance, although still from above the stage*]

Good-by George! Thank you for your services. Enjoy the rewards: enjoy your perfect woman... Good-bye Gaia! Enjoy your lust and germ-covered Planet Earth. Good-bye to all of you, imbeciles!

[*Loud ringing noise. Similar to a fire alarm, but not exactly like that. It sounds for a fifteen seconds, gradually becoming weaker and weaker*]

GAIA: James doesn't care, George. I keep repeating: he came here to sow the seeds of doubt, which can eventually lead to revolt... to revolution... and to improvement of humanity... and to its self-sufficiency. He calculated that if religions disappear, so will the wars, racism, poverty and ignorance! If humanity moves forward, James will be able to commit suicide. Maybe all of us will. Finally! I went ahead of them... I have chosen the sweetest form of suicide possible: I have chosen to live and die as a human being!

GEORGE: James wants us – humans – to become like you – Elidians – so all of you would be able to die! How absurd!

1st PATIENT: [*Giggling, pointing finger at George*]

Absurd...

[*Another long outburst of giggle*]

He said absurd!

GAIA: But all that matters is that I decided to stay. I decided to stay with you. I know you will desire me forever... Don't try to hide it; I know... And I want to do it now... here... in front of everybody.

[Slowly begins lifting up her skirt. All patients freeze, looking mesmerized at GAIA. She changes her mind and kneels in front of GEORGE. Her hands begin to move towards his fly, her full red lips slowly opening]

GEORGE: [*Suddenly raises his hands towards the ceiling... howling desperately*]

James, why have you forsaken me?!

BLACKOUT

END

Plays

Andre Vltchek

ABOUT THE AUTHOR

Novelist, filmmaker, investigative journalist, poet, playwright, and photographer, Andre has covered dozens of war zones and conflicts from Bosnia and Peru to Sri Lanka, DR Congo and Timor Leste.

He is the author of a novel Nalezeny, published in Czech. Point of No Return is his major work of fiction written in English and translated and published in French by Edition Yago. Other works include a book of political nonfiction Western Terror: From Potosi to Baghdad (translated into Turkish and published by Bilim + Gonul). Pluto publishing house in London recently published his provocative and critical book on Indonesia: Archipelago of Fear. Together with Rossie Indira, he is responsible for a book of conversations with the foremost Southeast Asian writer Pramoedya Ananta Toer, Exile (translated into Korean, Spanish and Bahasa Indonesia). Non-fiction book Oceania (published by Expathos) is a result of his five years work in Micronesia, Polynesia and Melanesia and a damning attack against neo-colonialism in the Pacific.

The plays Ghosts of Valparaiso and Conversations with James were translated into several languages including Spanish.

He has collaborated with UNESCO in Vietnam, Africa and Oceania through various publications including fiction books The Story of Ann and The Story of Moana. Presently he is finishing writing his monumental political novel Winter Journey.

He is a Senior Fellow at The Oakland Institute.

He writes and photographs for several publications worldwide, corporate and progressive, including RT, CounterPunch, Z Magazine, Newsweek, Asia Times, People's Daily, China Daily, Irish Times, A2 and Asia-Pacific Journal (Japan Focus).

He produced the feature length documentary film about the Indonesian massacres in 1965 "Terlena – Breaking of The Nation', as well as the film on the biggest refugee camp in the world Dadaab 'One Flew Over Dadaab'. His feature documentary film 'Rwandan Gambit' is reversing the official narrative on 1994, exposing Rwandan and Ugandan plunder of DR Congo on behalf of Western imperialism. His Japanese crew recently filmed his lengthy debate with Noam Chomsky on the state of the world which is presently being made into a film and a book. He is working on several new documentaries in Asia, Africa, and Latin America.

He frequently speaks at major universities, including Columbia, Cornell, Oxford, Cambridge, Sydney, Hong Kong, Auckland and Melbourne. Cofounder and Coeditor of Mainstay Press and Liberation Lit, he presently lives in Asia and Africa.

His website is:
http://andrevltchek.weebly.com/

And his twitter is: @AndreVltchek

Andre Vltchek

COMPLIMENTS FOR ANDRE VLTCHEK

"Andre Vltchek tells us about a world that few know, even when they think they do. That is because he tells the truth, vividly, with a keen sense of history, and with a perceptive eye that sees past surfaces to reality..." ~ *Noam Chomsky*

"Vltchek has written a colorful and elegantly crafted novel with a political stance that will engage some and provoke others but is always heart-felt and sincere." ~ *Lila Rajiva*

"André Vltchek is a writer, the real thing, of the same calibre and breed as Hemingway and Malraux." ~ *Catherine Merveilleux*

"André Vltchek offers an unsparing portrait of the world we live in. With his provocative outlook, he lays bare a situation that is really quite simple, and did not begin yesterday: a small group of nations whose economic system has nothing to do with humanism, solidarity or compassion, governs the world, exploiting the poorest

countries, making a mockery along the way of the democratic principles humanity has been struggling to uphold for centuries. He also recounts the innumerable excesses that accrue as a result, and touches on the subject of religion, which teaches submission."
Françoise Bachelet

"A serious piece of writing endowed with great sincerity, portraying a unique life experience that leaves us feeling forlorn even as it pulls us along in its wake."
Nathalie Zylberman

"Once again, it's the context that makes the book. It is quite simply mind-boggling. Andre Vltchek knows very well what he's talking about..." *Yves Mabon*

"Reading this book prompts certain reflections: to what degree can one be a witness and remain uninvolved, without being responsible? (...) An instructive and brilliant book that forces the reader to face the question: What sort of world are we leaving to our children? How could we ever justify ourselves? How far are we willing to go to change it?" *Valérie Revelut*

"Vltchek, previously unknown to me, consistently and calmly held his own during the conversations, speaking with comparable authority and knowledge about an extraordinary assortment of topics that embraced the entire global scene, something few of us would have the nerve to attempt, much less manage with such verve, insight, and empathy." *Richard A. Falk*

"...despite all the terror and despite somber analyses about the battle between 'market fundamentalists and religious fundamentalists' being the main contradiction of our time, Vltchek's novel projects the same desperate hope that once emanated from *Man's Fate* by André Malraux or *To Whom the Bells Toll* by Ernest Hemingway, and it is presumably not by accident that French critic Catherine Merveilleux has compared Vltchek with these very same authors. And as a matter of fact, Vltchek evokes strong memories of them, but not just because of his reawakening of the buried tradition of political fiction, but also because of his immense narrative talent." *Michael Schiffmann*

"Andre Vltchek is one of a few noble knights of investigative journalism. He travels to all the dangerous places in the world, "speaks truth to the power," and reports on the events on the ground. All of this in the hope people could open their eyes and minds and learn the seemingly incongruent fact that there are millions and millions of innocents, people like you and me, who were and still are being sacrificed in the name of the western-style democracy." ~ *Alevtina Rea*

Andre Vltchek

www.ingramcontent.com/pod-product-compliance
Lightning Source LLC
Chambersburg PA
CBHW031317160426
43196CB00007B/564